THE WOMAN'S BOOK
EVERYTHING BUT THE KITCHEN SINK

Francesca Beauman

WEIDENFELD & NICOLSON
LONDON

First published in Great Britain in 2007
by Weidenfeld & Nicolson

1 3 5 7 9 10 8 6 4 2

This book contains some lighthearted observations on a number of issues
and we hope you will enjoy it; however, the publishers and the author do not
hold the book out as the definitive guide to any of the subjects contained
within it. As with all guides, the suggestions herein should be approached
with common sense.

Particularly, while it tries to suggest ways of dealing with a number of
emergencies, it is not a medical text book and the way to approach and deal
with any of the emergencies must depend on the circumstances.

For medical matters, it is always sensible to seek medical advice as soon
as it becomes apparent that matters might get out of control. Do not believe
that this book can replace specialist advice.

A CIP catalogue record for this book is available from the British Library

ISBN 978 0 297 85271 1

Designed by Ben Cracknell Studios
Illustrations Ruth Murray
Printed in Great Britain

Weidenfeld & Nicolson
An imprint of the Orion Publishing Group
Orion House, 5 Upper St Martin's Lane, London WC2H 9EA

www.orionbooks.co.uk

THE WOMAN'S BOOK

Also by Francesca Beauman
The Pineapple: King of Fruits

Acknowledgements

'Diamonds Are a Girl's Best Friend', words by Leo Robin, music by Jule Styne © 1949 (Renewed) Consolidated Music Publishers Incorporated/Music Sales Corporation/Dorsey Brothers Music, USA. Dorsey Brothers Music Limited. Used by permission of Music Sales Limited. All Rights Reserved. International Copyright Secured.

Excerpt from *A Room of One's Own* by Virginia Woolf reprinted by permission of The Society of Authors as the Literary Representatives of the Estate of Virginia Woolf.

Definition of rain from *Oxford English Dictionary* ©1989 edited by Simpson, J. & Weiner, E. By permission of Oxford University Press.

Dorothy Parker quote reproduced by permission of Pollinger Limited and the proprietor as the Literary Representatives of the Estate of Dorothy Parker.

Extract from *Forever Summer* by Nigella Lawson, published by Chatto & Windus. Reprinted by permission of The Random House Group Ltd.

Excerpt from 'The Beggar at the Manor' from *The Odyssey* by Homer, translated by Robert Fitzgerald ©1961, 1963 by Robert Fitzgerald. Copyright renewed 1989 by Benedict R.C. Fitzgerald, on behalf of the Fitzgerald children. Reprinted by permission of Benedict R.C. Fitzgerald.

Diagram from the *Stern Review* reproduced under the terms of the Click-Use Licence.

Extract from *Downhill All the Way* by Leonard Woolf reproduced by permission of the University of Sussex and The Society of Authors as the Literary Representative of the Estate of Leonard Woolf.

Table of native British plants reproduced by kind permission of Professor Colin Spence.

Quote from *Modern Manners* (London, Hamlyn, 1992) by Drusilla Beyfus reproduced by kind permission of Drusilla Beyfus.

Quote from *Self-Consciousness* (New York, Knopf, 1989) by John Updike reproduced by kind permission of John Updike.

Diagram based on figure 1.1 in *Guns, Germs and Steel* (London, Jonathan Cape, 1997) by Jared Diamond reproduced by kind permission of Jared Diamond.

Every effort has been made to contact the copyright holders of the illustrations reproduced in this book and any omissions will be restituted at the earliest opportunity.

List of contents

Bras

....

T-shirt

Trainer/triangle

Balconette

Sports

Halterneck

Nursing

Push-up

Backless

Chicken fillet

No bra

Women in Malawi

....

	Malawi	UK
Total female population	6,621,100	30,588,700
Life expectancy	40	81
Female literacy	54%	99%
Women with HIV	7.6%	0.07%
Average age of women at marriage	19	34
Women who use contraception	30.6%	84.0%
Annual number of deaths in childbirth per 100,000	1800	13
Average number of children per woman	6.1	1.7
Likelihood of a girl attending primary school	99%	99%
Likelihood of a girl attending secondary school	23%	97%
Maternity leave	8 weeks at 100% full pay	26 weeks at 90% full pay
Female members of parliament	14%	20%

Source: United Nations Statistics Division

The most popular girls' names over the past one hundred years

....

	1904	1934	1964	1994	Today
1st	Mary	Margaret	Susan	Rebecca	Jessica[1]
2nd	Florence	Jean	Julie	Lauren	Emily
3rd	Doris	Mary	Karen	Jessica	Sophie
4th	Edith	Joan	Jacqueline[2]	Charlotte	Olivia
5th	Dorothy[3]	Patricia	Deborah	Hannah	Chloe

1 Jessica is originally a Hebrew name from the Old Testament meaning 'He sees', 'God's Grace' or 'wealthy'. It was first used in its current form by William Shakespeare in *The Merchant of Venice* for the daughter of a Jewish merchant.

2 The popularity of the name in the 1960s was due to Jacqueline Kennedy – who, for her outdoor wedding breakfast in Newport, Rhode Island to celebrate her marriage to John F. Kennedy, served her guests a dish of pineapple salad presented in a pineapple shell. Not recommended.

3 Famous Dorothys include Dorothy Wordsworth (William's sister), Dorothy Parker, Dorothy Dandridge, Dorothy L. Sayers, Dorothy Hodgkin, Dorothy Gale and Dorothy Perkins – a shop, not a person, but an essential cultural reference point nonetheless.

All hail vinegar

....

Dancer Margot Fonteyn defined magic as 'genius'. To playwright and poet Ntozake Shange, magic was 'woman'. To others – the clever ones – magic is vinegar. The use of vinegar for a range of household chores sounds like the sort of instruction that one's grandmother submitted to in the war only because she had no other choice. Fiddlesticks to that. In fact, it actually works – brilliantly, and without making the whole house reek of the stuff. It is also a thousand times cheaper and a million times more eco-friendly than commercial products.

N.B. Unless otherwise stated, distilled white vinegar is advised for cleaning and apple cider vinegar for health and beauty. Pour it into a spray bottle first to make it easier to use. As with every remedy it is worth testing its use on an inconspicuous corner of any material first, just to check that it has no adverse effect.

Uses

- *Window cleaner.* Dilute with four parts water.

- *Fabric softener*. Add about half a cup to the wash, just as one would with conventional fabric softener.

- *Air freshener*. Mix together two tablespoons of vinegar, two cups of water, and a teaspoon of baking soda (another magic creation) then spray into the air. Do not be alarmed when it foams a little – this will not last too long. Alternatively, pour it into a bowl and leave it lying around – that is, as long as you are not worried that guests might mistake it for dog pee.

- *Stain remover*. Mix together half vinegar and half water, then spray it on the stain in question, again just as one would with conventional stain remover, before you put the garment in the washing machine.

- *Weed killer*. Pour straight on to the weedy patch. It sometimes needs a couple of applications.

- *Loo cleaner*. Pour in, then leave overnight.

- *Treatment for stings*. Especially if stung by a Portuguese man-of-war (see page 92).

- *Drain cleaner*. Pour in, then leave overnight, both to remove smells and unclog (small) blockages.

- *Wallpaper remover*. Once the top layer of wallpaper has been removed, spray on some vinegar and leave it for a couple of minutes. The backing should then pull away relatively easily.

Scrape the excess glue off the wall, wipe the remaining glue away with vinegar, then rinse with water.

- *Nit remover*. Dip a comb in vinegar, then go to work on the hair as usual. It works by helping to break down the glue that nits use to cling on. It will also, incidentally, give the hair a welcome shininess by neutralising the alkali consistency of most shampoos.

- *Grease cutter.* Use straight vinegar to clean the oven, grill and hob. Spray on, leave for a few minutes, then wipe off.

- *Treatment for sunburn*. Soak a towel in a mixture of half vinegar and half water. It may sting a little at first, but it will eventually ease the pain and prevent blistering. The result is worth it. This also works with other types of mild burns.

- *Furniture polish*. Mix together equal parts of vinegar and vegetable oil, then apply with a soft cloth.

- *Limescale remover*. Soak a paper towel in vinegar, then use an elastic band to secure it over the area to be treated. Left overnight, the limescale will be easy to wipe away in the morning. This sometimes works even more effectively when the vinegar is boiled first.

- *Ear cleaner*. Mix together one third vinegar, one third water and one third rubbing alcohol, then pour it into a (clean) dropper bottle for use whenever. After application, the ear should be cleaned with a tissue after a couple of minutes. The technique also works on cats and dogs to prevent ear infections.

- *Insect repellent*. Just spray. It works on all kinds of insects. Ticks particularly hate it. Try pouring vinegar down any openings that ants find to sneak into the house – they will soon find some other, more hospitable home to visit. One's horse may also benefit – add five teaspoons of the cider kind to the horse's oats every morning and evening to reduce fly bites.

- *Show-shine enhancer*. Mix together half a cup of vinegar with about two pints of water, then spray on to a horse or a dog to make its coat gleam. It also helps prevent infections.

- *Glue solvent*. Apply vinegar to the area, leaving it to soak until results are seen. Be warned, though – this might take a while.

- *In red cabbage*. Much underrated. See page 101 for the recipe. Even those who claim not to like cabbage like this dish – even if they don't know it yet. Especially successful at Christmas-time.

- *Brass cleaner*. Mix together one part vinegar with ten parts water, then soak brass as necessary.

All hail vinegar

- *Treatment for alopecia*. Pour vinegar on the head, then wrap in a hot towel and leave overnight. Repeat every night until some improvement is seen.

- *Rust remover*. Soak the offending article in a bowl of vinegar for as long as necessary. (This works better on bolts than on cars . . .)

- *Rinse aid*. Fill the rinse-aid dispenser with vinegar just as one would with commercial rinse-aid products.

- *Denture cleaner*. Soak dentures in vinegar for about half an hour or as long as one would with commercial denture cleaner, then brush thoroughly.

- *Fish-tank cleaner*. Soak a cloth in vinegar, then wipe all the way around the inside of the tank where white mineral deposits tend to accumulate. Be assured that the vinegar is harmless to fish.

- *Chips enhancer*. Pour on liberally, ideally when drunk.

Magic indeed.

Winners of a Best Actress Oscar©

1927–8	Janet Gaynor	*Seventh Heaven*
1928–9	Mary Pickford	*Coquette*
1929–30	Norma Shearer	*The Divorcee*
1930–31	Marie Dressler	*Min and Bill*
1931–32	Helen Hayes	*The Sin of Madelon Claudet*
1932–33	Katharine Hepburn	*Morning Glory*
1934	Claudette Colbert	*It Happened One Night*
1935	Bette Davis	*Dangerous*[1]
1936	Luise Rainer	*The Great Ziegfeld*
1937	Luise Rainer	*The Good Earth*
1938	Bette Davis	*Jezebel*
1939	Vivien Leigh	*Gone With The Wind*
1940	Ginger Rogers	*Kitty Foyle*
1941	Joan Fontaine	*Suspicion*
1942	Greer Garson	*Mrs Miniver*[2]
1943	Jennifer Jones	*The Song of Bernadette*

1 'An actor is something less than a man; an actress is more than a woman,' read the inscription on Bette Davis's cigarette case.
2 Greer Garson's win holds the record for the longest acceptance speech ever given at an Academy Awards. It lasted approximately seven minutes.

All hail vinegar

1944	Ingrid Bergman	*Gaslight*
1945	Joan Crawford	*Mildred Pierce*
1946	Olivia de Havilland	*To Each His Own*
1947	Loretta Young	*The Farmer's Daughter*
1948	Jane Wyman	*Johnny Belinda*
1949	Olivia de Havilland	*The Heiress*
1950	Judy Holliday	*Born Yesterday*
1951	Vivien Leigh	*A Streetcar Named Desire*
1952	Shirley Booth	*Come Back, Little Sheba*
1953	Audrey Hepburn	*Roman Holiday*
1954	Grace Kelly	*The Country Girl*
1955	Anna Magnani	*The Rose Tattoo*
1956	Ingrid Bergman	*Anastasia*
1957	Joanne Woodward	*The Three Faces of Eve*
1958	Susan Hayward	*I Want To Live!*
1959	Simone Signoret	*Room At The Top*
1960	Elizabeth Taylor	*Butterfield 8*
1961	Sophia Loren	*Two Women*
1962	Anne Bancroft	*The Miracle Worker*
1963	Patricia Neal	*Hud*
1964	Julie Andrews	*Mary Poppins*
1965	Julie Christie	*Darling*
1966	Dame Elizabeth Taylor	*Who's Afraid Of Virginia Woolf?*
1967	Katharine Hepburn	*Guess Who's Coming To Dinner?*
1968 (tie)	Katharine Hepburn; Barbra Streisand	*The Lion In Winter; Funny Girl*[3]
1969	Maggie Smith	*The Prime Of Miss Jean Brodie*
1970	Glenda Jackson	*Women In Love*
1971	Jane Fonda	*Klute*
1972	Liza Minnelli	*Cabaret*
1973	Glenda Jackson	*A Touch Of Class*
1974	Ellen Burnstyn	*Alice Doesn't Live Here Anymore*
1975	Louise Fletcher	*One Flew Over The Cuckoo's Nest*
1976	Faye Dunaway	*Network*
1977	Diane Keaton	*Annie Hall*
1978	Jane Fonda	*Coming Home*
1979	Sally Field	*Norma Rae*
1980	Sissy Spacek	*Coal Miner's Daughter*
1981	Katharine Hepburn	*On Golden Pond*
1982	Meryl Streep	*Sophie's Choice*

3 The two actresses received 3030 votes each – the only exact tie in the history of the Oscars©.

Winners of a Best Actress Oscar©

1983	Shirley MacLaine	*Terms Of Endearment*
1984	Sally Field	*Places In The Heart*
1985	Geraldine Page	*The Trip to Bountiful*[4]
1986	Marlee Matlin	*Children Of A Lesser God*
1987	Cher	*Moonstruck*
1988	Jodie Foster	*The Accused*
1989	Jessica Tandy	*Driving Miss Daisy*
1990	Kathy Bates	*Misery*
1991	Jodie Foster	*The Silence Of The Lambs*
1992	Emma Thompson	*Howards End*
1993	Holly Hunter	*The Piano*
1994	Jessica Lange	*Blue Sky*
1995	Susan Sarandon	*Dead Man Walking*
1996	Frances McDormand	*Fargo*[5]
1997	Helen Hunt	*As Good As It Gets*
1998	Gwyneth Paltrow	*Shakespeare In Love*
1999	Hilary Swank	*Boys Don't Cry*
2000	Julia Roberts	*Erin Brockovich*
2001	Halle Berry	*Monster's Ball*
2002	Nicole Kidman	*The Hours*
2003	Charlize Theron	*Monster*
2004	Hilary Swank	*Million Dollar Baby*
2005	Reese Witherspoon	*Walk The Line*
2006	Helen Mirren	*The Queen*

4   Geraldine Page was so surprised when it was announced that she had won the award for Best Actress that before she went up on stage to receive it, she had to scrabble around for a while to find her shoes, which she had kicked off underneath her seat.

5   Frances McDormand was the first person to win for a film directed by a spouse (Joel Coen), though others have been similarly nominated: Gena Rowlands for *A Woman Under the Influence* (directed by husband John Cassavetes), Melina Mercouri for *Never on Sunday* (directed by husband Jules Dassin) and Julie Andrews for *Victor, Victoria* (directed by husband Blake Edwards).

Memorable film lines of the 1930s through to the 1970s

....

'I want to be alone.'
Grand Hotel (1932)

'Oh no, it wasn't the airplanes. It was Beauty killed the Beast.'
King Kong (1933)

'Toto, I've a feeling we're not in Kansas anymore.'
The Wizard of Oz (1939)

'As God is my witness, I'll never be hungry again.'
Gone With The Wind (1939)

'We'll always have Paris.'
Casablanca (1942)

'Oh, Jerry, don't let's ask for the moon. We have the stars.'
Now, Voyager (1942)

'We're neither of us free to love each other. There's too much
in the way. There's still time, if we control ourselves and behave
like sensible human beings. There's still time.'
Brief Encounter (1945)

'Story of my life. I always get the fuzzy end of the lollipop.'
Some Like It Hot (1959)

'That's the way it crumbles... cookie-wise.'
The Apartment (1960)

'All of you! You all killed him! And my brother, and Riff. Not
with bullets, or guns, with hate. Well now I can kill, too, because
now I have hate!'
West Side Story (1961)

'Love means never having to say you're sorry.'
Love Story (1970)

'Your girl is lovely, Hubbell.'
The Way We Were (1973)

Lonely-Hearts advertisements

In July 1695, alongside the advertisements for a cobbler's apprentice,
an Arabian stallion and a second-hand bed that appeared on page
three of the popular weekly pamphlet *A Collection for Improvement
of Husbandry and Trade*, the first ever Lonely-Hearts advertisement
was published:

> A Gentleman about 30 Years of Age, that says he had
> a Very Good Estate, would willingly Match himself to
> some Good Young Gentlewoman, that has a Fortune of
> 3000*l.* or thereabouts, and he will make Settlement to
> Content.

Henceforth, the Lonely-Hearts pages were to become a significant
player in the history of courtship in Britain.

If the beauteous Fair One who was in the front boxes at the play *Romeo and Juliet* last Wednesday night, dressed in a pink satin gown with a work'd handkerchief on, and a black feather in her hair with bugles, has a soul capable of returning a most sincere and ardent love to one who thinks he had the honour of being taken notice of by her as he sat in the side box; let her with all the frankness of a Juliet appoint in the paper or any other when, how and where she will give her Romeo a meeting.

Morning Chronicle, 1772

Matrimony. A Young Lady blessed with every advantage of affluence and beauty, and possessing all those agreeable qualities so often sought for in her sex, and so seldom found, is desirous of freeing herself from the control of a cruel and capricious Guardian: she therefore informs the public, that she would, without reluctance, throw herself into the arms of a man of spirit, who would affront danger, to rescue her from so irksome a confinement . . .

Public Advertiser, 1781

An agreeable and accomplished Woman would be glad to engage herself with a Single Gentleman. The reason of this public application is that the Lady is almost a stranger in this metropolis. A line addressed to X.I.F. to be left at the office of this Paper, will be answered immediately.

Morning Chronicle , 1789

I, John Hobnall, am at this writing five and forty, a widower, and in want of a wife. I have a good cottage with a couple of acres of land, for which I pay £2 a year. I have five children, four of them old enough to be in employment, three sides of bacon, and some pigs ready for market. I should like to have a woman fit to take care of her house when I am out . . . A good sterling woman would be preferred, who would take care of the pigs.

Blackwood, 1837

The advertiser, who has been much abroad, has no relations, feels lonely, and possesses a good round sum for the matrimonial cash-box, wishes to find a single or widow lady in a similar position, having a wish to marry. As to personal attractions, an interview is best to satisfy. He is genteel, of studious habits, gentle temper, neat in dress, and fond of travelling. Not exact as to age. Would prefer a plain, neat lady, rather than a dashy person . . . Address to R. Daron, 193 Bishopsgate-street Without, London.

News of the World, 1851

To Girls of Fortune – Matrimony. A bachelor, young, amiable, handsome, and of good family, and accustomed to move in the highest sphere of society, is embarrassed in his circumstances. Marriage is his only hope of extrication.

The Times, 1852

Wanted – by a young lady, aged nineteen, of pleasing countenance, good figure, agreeable manners, general information and varied accomplishments, who has studied every thing, from the creation to crochet, a situation in the family of a gentleman. She will take the head of the table, manage his household, scold his servants, nurse his babies (when they arrive), check his tradesmen's bills, accompany him to the theatre, cut the leaves of his new book, sew on his buttons, warm his slippers, and generally make his life happy. Apply in the first place, by letter, to Louisa Caroline, Linden Grove, London, and afterward to Papa, upon the premises.

The Times, 1873

The heir of an old country family (eight hundred years old, royal Norman descent), aged twenty-two, five feet nine inches, dark, very handsome eyes, a poet, highly talented, passionately fond of science and the fine arts, and of beauty in every shape, intends soon to enter Parliament. Would any lady correspond? Not over twenty-five, of good family, handsome, and with not less than £300 a year.

Matrimonial Journal, 1878

Lilian, Gladys and Rosalie, daughters of a deceased officer, have good incomes, ages 22, 20 and 18, don't want to die old maids . . .

Matrimonial News, 1885

In more recent times, it has become entirely acceptable to meet someone via a Lonely-Hearts advertisement, either in a newspaper or on the Internet. Anyone who thinks otherwise is not only wrong, but also stupid. It is an essential tool in the modern courtship process, and not to be mocked.

Internet courtship

To ease the inevitable awkwardness of a first attempt at courtship over the Internet, there are a few guidelines to follow. Do not be daunted by the number of websites that exist to facilitate the process; however, it is important to weigh the options up carefully. Just as the type of bar one goes to dictates the type of man one meets, so too does the type of website. To meet a thirty-five-year-old man who works in the media or the public sector, go to guardiansoulmates.co.uk. To meet a fifty-five-year-old man who works in finance or law, try onlylunch.co.uk. Simply to cast the net as widely as possible, go to datingdirect.com or match.com, two of the largest Internet dating sites in the country.

Be circumspect when composing or responding to an ad. A University of Liverpool study revealed that what people look for relates closely to men and women's evolutionary instincts.

Women's preferences:	Men's preferences:
1. Commitment	1. Attractiveness
2. Social skills	2. Commitment
3. Resources	3. Social skills
4. Attractiveness	4. Resources

It is important to be sufficiently broad-minded in terms of demands made early on. Placing an advertisement in which a dislike is professed for 'short men', 'men with glasses' or 'men with small hands' reveals oneself as the sort of person who treats men like made-to-measure curtains. This is to be avoided. There is no way of predicting who one is going to fall in love with, and a huge number of people end up rather surprising themselves with their ultimate choice of partner; thus, it would be foolish to narrow down the options too soon.

Once a potential match surfaces, exchange photographs as soon as possible. Do not tell too many lies. Email each other for a sufficient length of time before arranging to meet; this avoids too many ghastly surprises when you finally do. It also ensures that there is at least one topic of conversation with which to open proceedings, for example 'how did that meeting go?' or 'did you manage to find your sister a birthday present?' . Be polite: stay for two drinks at least. Refrain from making phone calls to girlfriends when you go to the loo. Finally, in terms of what to wear . . . if in doubt, overdress. This applies generally, in fact.

Lonely-Hearts abbreviations:

LTR – long-term relationship	W/E – well-endowed
GSOH – good sense of humour	MBA – married but available
WLTM – would like to meet	VGL – very good looking (not to be confused with VPL – visible panty line)
N/S – non-smoker	
S/A – straight acting	
ALAWP – all letters answered with photo	NSA – no strings attached
	ND – non-drinker
OHAC – own house and car	TDH – tall, dark and handsome
BDSM – bondage, domination, sadism and masochism	WTR – willing to relocate

As Nancy Mitford put it so succinctly in *The Pursuit of Love*: 'Wooing, so tiring'.

Getting married

....

Alice laughed: 'There's no use trying,' she said; 'one can't believe impossible things.'
    'I daresay you haven't had much practice,' said the Queen. 'When I was younger, I always did it for half an hour a day. Why, sometimes I've believed as many as six impossible things before breakfast.'
            Lewis Carroll, *Alice Through the Looking Glass* (1872)

It is a well-known statistic that approximately one in three marriages end in divorce. Yet, since 2002, marriage rates have been rising for the first time since 1972, when they reached an all-time high – a total of 480,285 such leaps of faith took place that year. It seems marriage is an institution that refuses to die out.

How to know whether or not to accept a proposal of marriage

In the modern world, simply being in love is not enough to make a relationship work. It is not even close to being enough, in fact. A whole host of other factors are involved, the most important of which is *timing*. This is depressing, unromantic even, but true. When it comes to marriage, it is especially true. The most eloquent proponent of this theory is that great commentator on modern times, Carrie Bradshaw. In her view, men are like taxis. They drive around all day picking up women; then one day, their light goes on all of a sudden, and boom!

They are ready to get married, and will simply marry the first woman who crosses their path thereafter whom they find at least vaguely acceptable.

To this end, a simple mathematical formula exists to help one ascertain whether or not to accept a proposal of marriage.

Let X=10, where X is the constant that the couple loves, likes and respects each other.

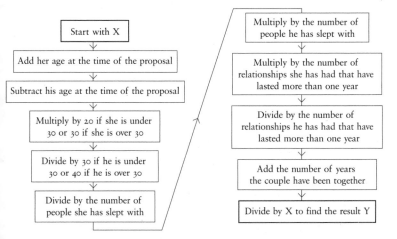

If Y > 0 but < 1, the couple should get married.

If Y < 0 or Y > 1, the couple should not get married.

NB: A small amount of leeway exists either way; so if Y=1.5, for example, that is acceptable.

If Y=0 exactly, however, the couple should definitely not get married, for revealed in this solution is the fact that at least one of the participants has either not had sex with anyone else but their intended, or has not had a long-term relationship with anyone else but their intended. In the age we live in, either scenario augers disaster in all but the most exceptional of couples.

Average cost of a wedding

NB: The percentages are more relevant than the actual costs since costs these days vary wildly from £200 to anywhere upwards of £200,000.

	£	%
Honeymoon	2,750	23.0
Food	2,200	18.0
Bride's dress	900	7.5
Engagement ring	850	7.0

Getting married

	£	%
Engagement party	750	6.2
Hire of venue	750	6.2
Drinks	700	5.8
Photography	400	3.4
Attendants outfits	400	3.4
Flowers	300	2.5
Video	275	2.3
Transport	250	2.1
Church fees	210	1.8
Groom's outfit	200	1.7
Bride's wedding ring	210	1.8
Cake	200	1.7
Stationery	180	1.5
Groom's wedding ring	175	1.5
Bride's going away outfit	150	1.3
First night hotel	150	1.3
Total:	12,000	100

Throughout the process, try to be guided by double Nobel Prize-winning scientist Marie Curie. In July 1895 she wore a simple navy-blue suit when she married Pierre Curie. She then wore this same suit to work in the laboratory every day for a decade or so. After all, the colour meant that it did not show the stains too much. This refusal to submit to the silliness of some of life's rituals expresses a way of looking at the world that is to be much admired and, as far as possible, emulated.

Mathematics

. . . .

'Sir Isaac Newton, though so deep in algebra and fluxions, could not readily make up a common account: and, when he was Master of the Mint, used to get somebody to make up his accounts for him.' So claimed Alexander Pope (1688–1744), the implication being that every one of us has our limitations. For many, mathematics is one of them. There is no doubt that much of the calculus and trigonometry one learns at school is limited in its usefulness; but other elements of mathematics are decidedly not. Yes, yes, one knows how to perform these mental machinations *in theory* – but in the heat of the moment, as one fights one's way to the next escalator at the John Lewis sale, how many of us are really so confident?

1. Percentages

The fraction method

How much of a reduction is 75% off an £80 John Lewis toaster?

Turn the 75% into a fraction – ¾. To work out what ¾ of £80 is, first work out what ¼ is (divide 80 by 4) then multiply this by 3.

The result? A reduction of £60. And a bargain.

The decimal method

If one invites 150 people to one's birthday party, how many are likely to refuse, given that the average refusal rate to invitations of this sort is approximately 30%?

Turn 30% into a decimal – 0.3. Then multiply 150 by 0.3.

Alternatively, cheat by first working out 10% of 150 – which is 15 – then multiplying the resulting figure by 3.

The result? 45 people are likely to refuse.

2. Probability

Probability is calculated as the number of successful outcomes divided by the total number of possible outcomes. Thus when playing craps at a Las Vegas casino at three in the morning in a sparkly frock, let it be known that the odds are as follows when two dice are thrown at the same time:

Total of the two dice	Odds against in a single toss
2	35 to 1
3	17 to 1
4	11 to 1
5	8 to 1
6	31 to 5 (or 6.2 to 1)
7	5 to 1
8	31 to 5 (or 6.2 to 1)
9	8 to 1
10	11 to 1
11	17 to 1
12	35 to 1

3. Volume

Just as the area of dance floor required to create a makeshift disco in one's very own home is calculated by multiplying the length of the room by the width of the room, similarly the volume of water required to fill the pond in the back garden enough to keep the koi content is calculated by multiplying the pond's length by its width by its depth or height. The result is measured in cubic centimetres or metres, bearing in mind that 1 cubic metre (m^3) is the same as 1,000,000 millilitres which is the same as 1,000 litres. The volume of an irregular-shaped object, such as a jug to be filled with Pimm's on a breezy summer's day, is much more complicated, involving a number of measurements calculated by finding one dimension of the object (e.g. its length), call that 'x', and the area of a cross section of the object, taken perpendicular to the known dimension. Find how the area of the cross section varies, as a function of its distance along x from one end, call that F(x). Take the integral of F(x) as x varies from 0 to the length of the object – by which time one rather deserves the whole jug to oneself, quite frankly.

4. Long division

Say the conundrum is how to divide a restaurant bill of £636 amongst 12 people (such a trial, and a mandate in itself against never going out to dinner in groups of more than 6). A number of cheat methods should be attempted before a calculator on a mobile telephone is produced (a terrible admission that one's brain is not quite as agile as it perhaps once was). Realistically, though, for a more complex sum this may well be the only option – in which case, at least keep the telephone under the table.

First, estimate a rough answer.

So 636÷12 is close to 600÷12, which is the same as 60÷12 plus a 0 i.e. 50 – plus a bit extra.

Next, there are various cheat options, depending on the numbers with which one is faced.

• Split the big number up

So 636÷12 is the same as (600÷12) + (36÷12), which is the same as 50 + 3, which is 53.

• Split the small number into factors

So 636÷12 is the same as 636÷2÷6, which is the same as 318÷6, which is 53.

• Keep dividing all the numbers in half for as long as possible

So 636÷12 is the same as 318÷6, which is the same as 159÷3, which is 53.

5. Long multiplication

Say the task at hand is to work out in one's head the number of times one has slept with one's husband during the eight years the two of you have been married – assuming it has averaged out at about once a week for each of the fifty-two weeks of the year, apart from, say, a total of seven weeks off due to being away for work, being too stressed at Christmas, being bitten by a tick in one's nether regions, and so forth.

Thus, the sum that faces one is 45 × 8. Again there are various cheat options:

• Multiply the tens then the units together

So 45x8 is the same as $(40 \times 8) + (5 \times 8)$, which is 360.

• Round up one number to the nearest 10 then adjust at the end

So 45x8 is the same as $(50 \times 8) - (5 \times 8)$, which is 360.

• Split it into factors

So 45×8 is the same as $45 \times 2 \times 2 \times 2$, which is 360.

When one is twenty years old, does one ever imagine that one will have sex with the same person 360 times? One does not.

Group sex

Popular combinations for group sex include:

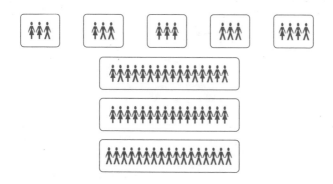

The etiquette of group sex varies considerably according to context. The main pitfalls to watch out for are outlined below.

In a private home (spontaneous)

In this scenario, the trickiest moment tends to occur when the idea of group sex is first proposed. Whomsoever it falls upon to do this places herself in a highly vulnerable position; hence, regardless of the response of the friends and/or acquaintances present, she is under no circumstances to be made to feel embarrassed or uncomfortable in any way. To be brave and open enough to suggest group sex in the first place is worthy of applause full stop. (She may just be drunk, however, or even high. Still.)

If group sex is your sort of thing, then chocs away. If, however, it happens not to be – which simply by the law of averages may well be the case – it is nonetheless important to respond to the suggestion politely and gracefully. Try to view it as akin to receiving an invitation to go pot-holing or to stroke someone's pet snake – one might not feel it is quite one's cup of tea, but it is always nice to be asked, and for that one should be appreciative. A simple 'gosh, what a lovely offer, but I'm OK actually' should suffice. (Either way, it is advisable to take a moment to think through what one's reaction would be if the opportunity ever presents itself. This prevents all manner of awkwardness that can arise from indecision).

If, on the other hand, you find yourself on the receiving end of a rebuff, it is proper to respond equally politely and gracefully – 'No problem. But if you ever change your mind . . .' The aim is to imply that the offer remains out there, yet without anyone feeling pressured. Then swiftly move the evening on – organise another round of drinks, suggest another round of bridge, begin a game of charades . . . whatever. Do not under any circumstances leave the gathering for at least thirty minutes after the suggestion has been made; to do so is to imply one is embarrassed, an entirely unwarranted sentiment assuming the others present have approached the situation in the proper way.

In a private home (pre-planned)

There are organisations that arrange for group sex to occur in a pre-planned manner. Some of these, such as Killing Kittens (killingkittens. co.uk), are specifically female-friendly. One advantage of this approach is that those involved do not generally know each other – though this could also be a disadvantage, of course.

Either way, this option allows one the opportunity to arrive prepared, and for a game plan to be worked out before diving on in. Elements of the game plan might include: know the boundaries; be accompanied by a trusted boyfriend, girlfriend or friend; bring protection; and so forth.

As with planting a new garden or doing the Christmas shopping, it is when, where and how to take the initial plunge that tends to be the most daunting element of the process. Remember that everyone is nervous. Initiate some conversation, though make sure this is kept to the impersonal: the weather, holiday destinations, and recent films or books all work well as topics to steer towards. If at any point you see someone you know from another context – whether from work, from the dry-cleaners, or from the pages of a magazine – be discreet. They too have the right to pursue and explore.

The moment will come when it is necessary – desirable, hopefully – to address the matter at hand. There is no getting away from the fact that at this point what one needs is a fair amount of chutzpah, coupled with a stiff drink.

Be assured that, actually, many of the usual rules of social interaction continue to apply in a group-sex scenario. Do not monopolise the handsomest man or woman at the party. Be generous with introductions. Make sure everyone feels included. At any point in the proceedings, feel free to approach those who interest or attract you. In the UK, as well as in Europe, it is acceptable in this context to touch someone in a non-sexual place as a form of non-verbal proposition; however, in the US, it is considered impolite to presume to touch someone without asking permission. If while engaged in sexual activity one is approached by someone who does not appeal just at that moment, simply raise a hand and say, 'We're OK, thanks'. Do not attempt to explain. Be polite to everyone, whether you find them attractive or not. After all, as a general rule, it is the uglier men who perform the best, simply because they have more to prove. On the other side, a rebuff of this sort is not to be taken personally. Either way, no means no.

And – obviously – always use protection.

At a sex club

Alternatively, there are so-called 'sex clubs', which are rather more public affairs. In the UK, these tend to be somewhat seedy places (though no doubt it is only a matter of time before this situation improves). Instead, a trip to Paris is recommended. There, sex clubs are a relatively well-accepted leisure activity akin to going to the cinema or strolling in the park. The city boasts nearly fifty such establishments, but some are inevitably chicer than others so it is important to choose carefully. Beginners should try Chris & Manu or L'Abys, two of the most mainstream and thus the least daunting. Most cater predominantly for couples or single women, and ban single men. Some include (an often surprisingly delicious) dinner in the price of entry.

Whatever the context, the codes of behaviour that govern the end of an evening of group sex are relatively similar. If one loses one's coat, one's bra or indeed any item of clothing, it is more polite to telephone the following day to enquire as to its whereabouts than to interrupt the host or hostess in whatever they are doing then and there. On taking one's leave, there is no need to say goodbye to everyone – only to those with whom you feel you have built up a particular rapport. And, finally, unlike almost every other sort of social gathering, there is no need to write a thank-you letter.

How to buy a swimming costume

....

Buying a swimming costume is one of the few areas of clothes shopping where it is simply counter-productive to be a stickler for perfection. Accept that never in the history of the universe has there existed a woman who has looked at herself in the changing-room mirror whilst wearing a swimming costume and thought, 'By golly, you look fabulous!' Ignore the images of the likes of Keira Knightly that promote twenty-first-century ideals of what constitutes the perfect body. Instead, focus on the following: air-brushing, air-brushing and air-brushing – the foremost reason a celebrity looks the way she does in any magazine. The only exceptions to this rule are Madonna (who spends three hours a day working at it, and thus deserves it) and Kate Moss (who doesn't, and doesn't).

The aim therefore, is simply to attempt to limit the trauma inflicted by the task at hand.

Preparation

Before embarking on the trip, take all the necessary steps towards whatever is a standard level of hair removal. If this means none, then fine. But if this means three hours with the lovely and brilliant Brazilian woman on the high street, so be it; otherwise it is inevitable that one will fail to look quite how one pictured oneself in one's head. Next, be broadminded in the choice of shop. Swimming costumes are not like shoes or bags – one does not get what one pays for. So it is worth trying anywhere from Hennes to Harvey Nichols.

The changing room

Once a selection has been made, the wisdom of Erma Bombeck comes into play: 'Women shop for a bikini with more care than they do a husband. The rules are the same. Look for something you'll feel comfortable wearing. Allow for room to grow.' Try to focus on the one aspect of your body that you like the most, then look for something that draws attention to it: bright colours, a pattern, a bow, a belt, embroidery, ruching or the like. Ensure the top half of the bikini sits comfortably; similarly, that the bottom half is not digging in anywhere. Also note that if the latter does not seem to be providing enough coverage, it is not a different size that is required, but a different design entirely. For advice on which style of swimming costume suits which particular body shape, simply pick up a copy of any woman's magazine in around June or July.

The decision

It is important to bear in mind when and where the swimming costume is most likely to be making an appearance. For surfing, a string bikini is off-limits. Ditto for kayaking down the Amazon. For lifeguards, a plain-coloured one-piece is mandatory. For the synchronised-swimming final at the Olympics, a one-piece is also recommended, but cosmetic matters should be factored into the equation: a gold or silver one is the ideal choice here. A thong bikini is acceptable on Copacabana beach in Rio de Janeiro – nowhere else. And, regardless of context, when it comes to swimming costumes, prevailing fashion trends are to be ignored entirely. The single exception to this is the one-piece, which is about to enjoy a significant renaissance. There are an increasing number of designs available that are the opposite of dull – with plunging necklines, cut-out waists, halter-necks and so on. For tall-ish women, something along these lines is the ideal choice. If all else fails, muddle through with the least ghastly option but distract the onlooker's eye upwards and away from the body with a spectacularly elaborate hairstyle. A 'Princess Leia' works particularly well for this purpose.

When it comes actually to donning the swimming costume, it is essential to remind oneself as often as possible that no one is looking. To reiterate, *no one* is looking. They are all far, far too preoccupied worrying about their own appearance – both the women and, increasingly, the men too.

How to clean a pearl necklace

Pearls were once so expensive that the Roman general Vitellius is said to have financed an entire military campaign by selling just one of his mother's pearl earrings. Historically, pearls were found naturally in oyster beds in the Persian Gulf, the Red Sea and along the coasts of India and Sri Lanka, but today most pearls tend to be cultured – encouraged into existence by humans, in other words.

Pearls should be cleaned every time they are worn. Merely by coming into contact with the skin, they absorb the acid it contains which over time has a harmful effect. Similarly, make-up, perfume and hairspray all cause them to deteriorate. Never use a commercial jewellery cleaner – these almost always contain undesirable amounts of ammonia. Instead, simply wipe each individual pearl with a very slightly damp cloth. About every fifth time they are worn, a more thorough cleaning is recommended. Use a soft cloth dipped in mild soapy water, *never* use washing-up liquid; then remove any soap residue with a different damp cloth and leave the necklace to dry. Store it in a silk, satin or velvet pouch (never a plastic one, which will cause the pearls to dry out and crack).

The personality of a beehive

How does one determine the personality of a beehive? The unenlightened may well consider this to be a preposterous question, but, in fact, the humble beehive is capable of a gamut of emotions. Not only are they most rewarding to explore from a philosophical and scientific point of view, but a sensitivity to the disposition of a beehive may also spare one unnecessary, and possibly painful, entanglements with the hive's occupants in the future.

The happy hive

Contrary to popular belief a happy hive does not wish to sting passers-by, and the ridiculous flailing and shrieking that commonly accompanies a human encounter with bees is entirely unwarranted. A hive is at its happiest when the air is warm and damp, as this is when bees fly the most easily and plants secrete the most nectar. Happy bees will also pursue an interloper (whether human or otherwise) no further than twelve feet from the hive. A hive betrays its contentment with a deep hum.

The euphoric swarm

The bee's greatest joy is the moment of 'swarming'. This is when the bees gorge themselves before setting off en masse with a queen to establish a new colony. This generally takes place at midday on a fine day, and is accompanied by a tremendous amount of noise. While the great boiling mass of bees may look threatening, it is in fact unlikely to attack as it has no home to protect. Should one encounter a swarm, however, the most sensible thing to do would be to telephone one's local beekeeping association to arrange for someone to collect the swarm, which is done by literally 'pouring' them into a box and taking them to a new home.

The unhappy hive

An unhappy hive expresses its discontent by emitting an agitated, high-pitched whine, and on these occasions it would be wise to steer well clear. During particularly stormy weather conditions, the hive is likely to be of a slightly worse disposition, as it appears that bees are upset by the electrical charge in the atmosphere. Rough handling or bumps from the beekeeper may also upset the colony, which may often retain an unhappy memory for up to a week at a time. Should the hive lose its queen, the colony will also fall into disarray and bad temper unless a new queen is found quickly, otherwise, as an absolute last resort, the colony must be put to death by pouring half a pint of petrol into the top of the hive.

The grief-stricken hive

By the early nineteenth century, the hive had attained something of the status of a family member in many European households. On the occasion of a death in the family, the ceremony of 'telling the bees' was enacted in the belief that this would prevent the grief-stricken bees from ceasing to produce honey, leaving the hive, or passing away altogether. Should one be fortunate enough to be in possession of a beehive, and unfortunate enough to lose a family member, one may consider it prudent to perform a similar ritual:

1. A family member or trusted servant raps the hive three times with the key of the household.

2. The hive is informed 'Your master is dead' followed by an entreaty not to leave.

3. The hive is dressed in a black crêpe bow.

4. The hive is supplied with food from the funeral gathering.

5. After an appropriate interval the hive is informed of the identity of its new master, ideally by way of a personal introduction.

A similar ceremony, replacing the black crêpe with something gayer such as a red cloth, may also be performed on the occasion of a family wedding.

Bee nationalities

While one does not like to be prejudiced about these things, nationality can play a key part in determining a bee's disposition. Some well-known types of bees include:

• *Italian Bee*. The large, plump and golden queen breeds gentle bees that produce plentiful honey.

• *British Black Bee*. Making something of a comeback, it is resilient to disease, but is also known for its 'sparky' character and a greater tendency to sting.

• *African Killer Bee*. Extremely plentiful honey producers but, as the name suggests, not a personality to be trifled with.

The personality of a beehive

Chocolate

The three foremost varieties of cocoa beans used in chocolate are criollo, trinitario and forastero. Of these, criollo is the rarest and most expensive cocoa on the market. A woman who professes not to like any of these – in other words, not to like chocolate – is generally deemed a freak, a liar or a man in drag. There is still debate about whether chocolate really is preferable to sex. For those who believe it is, see page 23 on group sex. Nonetheless, there is no doubt that it is a marvellous creation.

The origin of the word chocolate is an amalgamation of the Aztec words *xocolli*, meaning 'bitter', and *atl*, meaning 'water'. Cocoa beans, from which chocolate derives, were initially imbibed in the form of a bitter drink, often with copious amounts of chilli added. This is not to be recommended. Christopher Columbus stumbled across cocoa beans in 1502 as he robbed a Mayan trading canoe that was carrying the beans as cargo. Columbus initially believed them to be a type of almond: 'They seemed to hold these almonds at a great price; for when they were brought onboard ship together with their goods, I observed that when any of these almonds fell, they all stooped to pick it up, as if an eye had fallen.' In fact, cocoa beans were once a common form of currency in South America.

The melting point of chocolate ranges from 17°C to 36°C, which is slightly below human body temperature (about 37°C). It is for this reason that it literally melts in your mouth. The British eat about ten

The provenance of the world's cocoa bean supply:

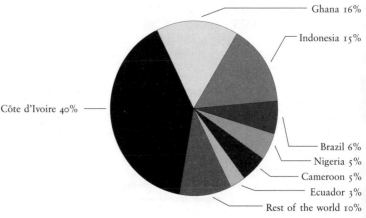

Ghana 16%

Indonesia 15%

Côte d'Ivoire 40%

Brazil 6%

Nigeria 5%

Cameroon 5%

Ecuador 3%

Rest of the world 10%

The chocolates found in a Prestat assortment box:

Chocolate ginger

Caramel

Rose Cream

Banoffee Truffle

Chocolate Truffle

Dark praline

kilograms of chocolate per person per year, making them the biggest consumers in Europe. The most delicious make is Prestat, which was established in 1902 and is still supplier to the Queen.

Finally, if one learns just one way to make chocolate cake – and after all, why learn more? – use the recipe in Nigella Lawson's *Nigella Bites* (Chatto and Windus 2001). Do not be daunted by the number of ingredients: the preparation technique is miraculously simple, and this is one recipe that turns out just dandy every single time.

Voting

Tales abound of strange creatures who choose to spend more than a single second of their precious time on earth in a dilemma over whether or not to vote. The more functioning members of the human race appreciate that this is a little like being in a dilemma about whether or not to breathe. To use a term coined by our some-time friends across the Pond – it is a no-brainer. Yet there are those who disagree, and who regularly fail to make it to the ballot box. Such behaviour may be considered perfectly reasonable by some, although one must assume that these people are content to accept the fact that for the next few years, they will have *no* right *whatsoever* to complain about any of the following: traffic wardens, bus routes, the bin men, schools, hospitals, crime, war and all the other thousands of issues that our elected representatives attend to. One must also assume that by abstaining, they are happy to forget the deaths, less than a hundred years ago, of scores of British women who fought for the right to vote. But for those who have the slightest trace of social/political/moral/ environmental/any conscience, there is simply no excuse not to make the journey to the polling station when required. Alternatively, one could register for a postal vote, then one need only find the nearest post box. For those who are unequal even to this tiny task, there is only one solution: get thee to Belarus! You do not deserve to live in a stable, democratic society.

Date women won the right to vote

Unless otherwise indicated, the date signifies the year women were granted the right both to vote and to stand for election.

* Right subject to conditions or restrictions
** Restrictions or conditions lifted

1788	United States of America (to stand for election)
1893	New Zealand (to vote)
1902	Australia*
1906	Finland
1907	Norway (to stand for election)*
1913	Norway**
1915	Denmark, Iceland*
1917	Canada (to vote)*, Netherlands (to stand for election)
1918	Austria, Canada (to vote)*, Estonia, Georgia, Germany, Hungary, Ireland*, Kyrgyzstan, Latvia, Lithuania, Poland, Russian Federation, United Kingdom (restricted to women over thirty)*
1919	Belarus, Belgium (to vote)*, Luxembourg, Netherlands (to vote), New Zealand (to stand for election), Sweden*, Ukraine
1920	Albania, Canada (to stand for election)*, Czechoslovakia, Iceland**, United States of America (to vote)
1921	Armenia, Azerbaijan, Belgium (to stand for election)*, Sweden**
1924	Kazakhstan, Mongolia, Saint Lucia, Tajikistan
1927	Turkmenistan
1928	Ireland**, United Kingdom (now included all women over twenty-one)**
1929	Ecuador*, Romania*
1930	South Africa ('Whites'), Turkey (to vote)
1931	Chile*, Portugal*, Spain, Sri Lanka
1932	Brazil, Maldives, Thailand, Uruguay
1934	Cuba, Portugal*, Turkey (to stand for election)
1937	Philippines
1938	Bolivia*, Uzbekistan
1939	El Salvador (to vote)
1941	Panama*
1942	Dominican Republic
1944	Bulgaria, France, Jamaica
1945	Croatia, Guyana (to stand for election), Indonesia, Italy, Japan, Senegal, Slovenia, Togo
1946	Cameroon, North Korea, Djibouti (to vote), Guatemala, Liberia, Panama**, Romania**, Trinidad and Tobago, Venezuela, Vietnam, Yugoslavia

1947	Argentina, Malta, Mexico (to vote), Pakistan, Singapore
1948	Belgium**, Israel, Niger, South Korea, Seychelles, Suriname
1949	Chile**, China, Costa Rica, Syria (to vote)*
1950	Barbados, Canada (to vote)**, Haiti, India
1951	Antigua and Barbuda, Dominica, Grenada, Nepal, Saint Kitts and Nevis, Saint Vincent and the Grenadines
1952	Bolivia**, Côte d'Ivoire, Greece, Lebanon
1953	Bhutan, Guyana (to vote), Mexico (to stand for election), Syria**
1954	Belize, Colombia, Ghana
1955	Cambodia, Eritrea, Ethiopia, Honduras, Nicaragua, Peru
1956	Benin, Comoros, Egypt, Gabon, Mali, Mauritius, Somalia
1957	Malaysia, Zimbabwe (to vote)**
1958	Burkina Faso, Chad, Guinea, Laos, Nigeria (South)
1959	Madagascar, San Marino (to vote), Tunisia, Tanzania
1960	Canada (to stand for election)**, Cyprus, Gambia, Tonga
1961	Bahamas*, Burundi, El Salvador (to stand for election), Malawi, Mauritania, Paraguay, Rwanda, Sierra Leone
1962	Algeria, Australia**, Monaco, Uganda, Zambia
1963	Afghanistan, Equatorial Guinea, Fiji, Iran, Kenya, Morocco, Papua New Guinea (to stand for election)
1964	Bahamas**, Libya, Papua New Guinea (to vote), Sudan
1965	Botswana, Lesotho
1967	Ecuador**, Kiribati, Tuvalu, Yemen
1968	Nauru, Swaziland
1970	Andorra (to vote), Yemen
1971	Switzerland
1972	Bangladesh
1973	Andorra (to stand for election), Bahrain, San Marino (to stand for election)
1974	Jordan, Solomon Islands
1975	Angola, Cape Verde, Mozambique, Sao Tome and Principe, Vanuatu
1976	Portugal**
1977	Guinea Bissau
1978	Nigeria (North), Zimbabwe (to stand for election)
1979	Marshall Islands, Micronesia, Palau
1980	Iraq
1984	Lichtenstein, South Africa ('Coloureds and Indians')
1986	Central African Republic, Djibouti (to stand for election)
1989	Namibia
1990	Samoa
1994	South Africa ('Blacks')
2005	Kuwait

NB Saudia Arabia is currently the only country where men are allowed to vote and women are not.

Source: Inter-Parliamentary Union (ipu.org)

Voting

There are no ifs, ands, buts or hanging chads about it – choosing not to exercise one's right to vote is sheer laziness. Many, however, attempt to justify abstention by arguing that, these days, Britain's three major political parties have shifted so closely together in terms of policy that there is nobody to vote for. The only sensible response to this is: grow up. If you feel there is nobody to vote for, then find someone to vote for. Go to meetings and propose a candidate you do like. All candidates need to have someone to propose them and someone to second them, both of whom must be registered voters within the relevant constituency. The nomination then has to be signed by eight or more registered voters and submitted along with a deposit of £500 (this is returned only if candidates receive more than 5 per cent of votes cast). So why not lobby a friend or acquaintance to stand?

Or even better, stand yourself. As long as you are over twenty-one and not insane, bankrupt, in prison or employed as a civil servant, a policeman, a member of the clergy or certain other positions of responsibility, then you are eligible to become an MP. To do this with the support of one of the major political parties, first you need to get involved with the party on a local level. Get elected as a councillor or a member of the school board to demonstrate your aptitude for politics. Then contact party HQ to register as a potential candidate. This sets off the selection process, which usually includes things like giving a speech to local party members, who then vote for their preferred candidate based on this and any other relevant factors.

Alternatively, you could start your own political party. Why not? Others have. For inspiration, below are a selection of some of the sixty-two parties (other than Labour, Conservative, and Liberal Democrats and its predecessors) that have fielded candidates between 1945 and 2001.

	No. of candidates	No. of MPs	Saved Deposits	Average % Vote
Anti-Partition of Ireland League of Great Britain				
1950	4	0	0	3.0
1951	1	0	0	2.7
British Empire Party				
1951	1	0	0	3.4
British National Party (1)				
1964	1	0	0	9.1
1966	3	0	0	5.3
British National Party (2)				
1983	54	0	0	0.5
1987	2	0	0	0.6
1992	13	0	0	1.2
1997	57	0	3	1.3
2001	33	0	5	3.9

	No. of candidates	No. of MPs	Saved Deposits	Average % Vote
Commonwealth				
1945	23	1	7	12.6
Communist Party of Great Britain				
1945	21	2	9	14.6
1950	100	0	3	2.0
1951	10	0	0	4.7
1955	17	0	2	4.9
1959	18	0	1	4.3
1964	36	0	0	3.5
1966	57	0	0	3.0
1970	58	0	0	1.8
1974 (Feb)[1]	44	0	1	1.8
1974 (Oct)	29	0	0	1.6
1979	35	0	0	0.8
1983	35	0	0	0.8
1987	19	0	0	0.7
1992	3	0	0	0.3
1997	3	0	0	0.4
2001	6	0	0	0.5
Ecology Party				
1979	51	0	0	1.5
1983	105	0	0	1.0
Green Party				
1987	133	0	0	1.4
1992	253	0	0	1.3
1997	94	0	1	1.2
2001	145	0	10	2.8
Independent Labour Party				
1945	5	3	4	35.2
1950	4	0	0	2.7
1951	3	0	0	3.6
1955	2	0	0	5.0
1959	2	0	0	1.8
1966	1	0	0	0.9
1970	1	0	0	1.7
Independent Nuclear Disarmament Election Committee				
1964	2	0	0	1.6
Islamic Party				
1992	4	0	0	0.6
League of Empire Loyalists				
1964	3	0	0	0.9

1 Two elections were held in 1974, one
   in February and one in October.

	No. of candidates	No. of MPs	Saved Deposits	Average % Vote
Legalise Cannabis				
1997	4	0	0	1.0
2001	13	0	0	1.6
Liverpool Protestant Group				
1945	1	0	0	13.2
Mebyon Kernow[2]				
1970	1	0	0	2.0
1974 (Feb)	1	0	0	1.5
1974 (Oct)	1	0	0	0.7
1979	2	0	0	3.5.
1983	2	0	0	1.2
1997	3	0	0	1.1
2001	3	0	0	2.1
Monster Raving Loony Party				
1983	11	0	0	0.7
1987	5	0	0	0.7
1992	22	0	0	0.6
1997	24	0	0	0.7
2001	15	0	0	1.0
Muslim Party				
2001	4	0	0	0.9
National Front				
1970	10	0	0	3.6
1974 (Feb)	54	0	0	3.1
1974 (Oct)	90	0	0	3.1
1979	303	0	0	1.3
1983	60	0	0	1.1
1992	14	0	0	0.8
1997	6	0	0	0.9
2001	5	0	0	1.5
Natural Law Party				
1992	309	0	0	0.5
1997	177	0	0	0.3
Patriotic Party				
1964	2	0	0	1.5
1966	1	0	0	0.4
Plaid Cymru				
1945	7	0	1	9.1
1950	7	0	1	6.8
1951	4	0	0	6.1
1955	11	0	4	11.3
1959	20	0	6	10.3
1964	23	0	2	8.4

2 Mebyon Kernow campaigns for greater self-government for Cornwall.

	No. of candidates	No. of MPs	Saved Deposits	Average % Vote
Plaid Cymru (*continued*)				
1966	36	0	2	8.7
1970	36	0	11	12.4
1974 (Feb)	36	2	10	11.7
1974 (Oct)	36	3	10	11.6
1979	36	2	8	8.6
1983	38	2	6	7.8
1987	38	3	18	7.3
1992	35	4	13	9.0
1997	40	4	25	9.9
2001	40	4	35	14.8
Pro-life Alliance				
1997	56	0	0	0.7
2001	37	0	0	0.7
Referendum Party				
1997	547	0	42	3.1
Scottish Militant Labour				
1992	1	0	1	19.3
Scottish National Party				
1945	8	0	2	9.1
1950	3	0	0	7.4
1951	2	0	1	10.0
1955	2	0	1	14.8
1959	5	0	2	11.3
1964	15	0	3	10.6
1966	23	0	13	14.1
1970	65	1	22	12.8
1974 (Feb)	70	7	63	22.7
1974 (Oct)	71	11	71	30.6
1979	72	2	54	17.2
1983	72	2	19	11.8
1987	71	3	70	14.1
1992	72	3	72	21.5
1997	72	6	72	22.1
2001	72	5	72	20.3
Socialist Labour Party				
1997	64	0	3	1.8
2001	114	0	1	1.4
Socialist Party of Great Britain				
1945	1	0	0	1.7
1950	2	0	0	0.6
1959	1	0	0	2.4
1964	2	0	0	0.5

	No. of candidates	No. of MPs	Saved Deposits	Average % Vote
Socialist Party of Great Britain *(continued)*				
1966	2	0	0	0.5
1970	2	0	0	0.6
1974 (Oct)	1	0	0	0.3
United Kingdom Independence Party				
1997	194	0	1	1.1
2001	428	0	6	2.1
Wessex Regional Party				
1979	7	0	0	0.7
1983	10	0	0	0.3
Workers Revolutionary Party				
1974 (Feb)	9	0	0	1.0
1974 (Oct)	10	0	0	0.9
1979	52	0	0	0.5
1983	21	0	0	0.4
1987	10	0	0	0.4
1992	2	0	0	0.4
1997	9	0	0	0.3
2001	6	0	0	0.3

Source: House of Commons Research Paper 04/61:
'UK Election Statistics: 1918–2004'

The terminology of sleeves

angel sleeve: a long, wide sleeve that flows loosely from the shoulder. The height of fashion in the fourteenth century.

armlet: a small, short sleeve shaped like a band around the arm.

bag sleeve: 1. A sleeve that is full to the elbow, tapering at the wrist, and gathered into a wide cuff. Popular in the early fifteenth century. 2. A sleeve that is narrow to the elbow, then bags from the elbow to the wrist. Also fifteenth century.

balloon sleeve: an extremely full, rounded sleeve, usually lined with buckram or some such fabric, that goes from shoulder to elbow (sometimes shoulder to wrist). Also known as a *melon sleeve*. A fad in the 1890s.

barrel sleeve: a barrel-shaped sleeve that tapers from the elbow, where it is at its widest, down to a narrow wrist and up to natural shoulder. Sometimes with a horizontal seam in the middle.

batwing sleeve, see *dolman sleeve*.

bell sleeve: a full sleeve that flares a little at the lower edge like a bell.

bernhardt sleeve: a long, fitted sleeve, usually with a point over the top of the wrist, with the fabric gathered into the lining in a *mousquetaire* fashion.

bishop sleeve: a long sleeve that is full in the lower part below the elbow like an Anglican bishop's robe, and either loose or held by a band at wrist. At the peak of its popularity around 1900.

bracelet sleeve: a sleeve that reaches below the elbow, about halfway to the wrist – convenient for wearing bracelets, in other words.

cape sleeve: a loose, full sleeve that hangs freely at the front and the back of the shoulder, like a cape.

cap sleeve: a short sleeve that just covers the shoulder, but does not continue underneath the arm.

cornet sleeve: a trumpet-shaped sleeve that ends in a low, bell-like flare.

cowl sleeve: a sleeve with a cowl drape at the shoulder.

cubital: a sleeve that only covers the arm from the wrist to the elbow. From the Latin word *cubitum*, meaning elbow.

dolman sleeve: a sleeve cut as an extension of the bodice of a dress, shirt, or jacket, designed without a socket for the shoulder, thus creating a deep, wide armhole that reaches from the waist to a narrowed wrist. Very fashionable in the 1920s and 1930s, in the 1980s then again in the 2000s, by which time it had also become known as a *batwing sleeve*.

double sleeve: a wide, sometimes flared oversleeve on top of a fitted undersleeve, often in a contrasting colour.

draped elbow sleeve: a straight sleeve that reaches to the elbow where it ends in a draped, loose fold to suggest a wide sleeve that has been turned back. Common in the seventeenth and eighteenth centuries.

elbow sleeve: a sleeve that extends to or slightly beyond the elbow.

envelope sleeve: a sleeve that is full at the shoulder, pleated in triangular folds.

foresleeve: 1. A section of a sleeve that covers the forearm. 2. An extra decorative sleeve. Often removable.

free action sleeve: a trade term for a type of sleeve that has an additional section under the arm that allows increased freedom of movement.

funnel sleeve: a sleeve shaped like a funnel, funnily enough, with the top turned back to form a cuff. An invention of the sixteenth century.

gigot: see *leg-of-mutton sleeve*.

goddess sleeve: a sleeve that billows out gracefully below the elbow, then is gathered in again twice before reaching the wrist. For the best examples of goddess fashion generally, refer to the near-perfect film *One Touch of Venus* (1948) starring Ava Gardner and Robert Walker.

half sleeve: 1. A removable mini-sleeve that only covers the forearm. Usually made of lace or sheer fabric. Worn for extra-warmth. 2. A sleeve protector worn by clerical workers.

hanging sleeve: a coat sleeve that hangs down at the side, but with a slit in the front for the arm itself to peep through. The arm was often then covered with an elaborately decorated shirt or blouse sleeve. Most popular in the fifteenth century.

kimono sleeve: an extra-large sleeve panel set into a deep armhole that extends from the shoulder to the waist.

lapped sleeve: a short sleeve with the fabric lapped backwards or forwards at the shoulder to give the effect of a fold.

leg-of-mutton sleeve: a sleeve shaped like a leg of mutton. It fits tightly from the wrist to the elbow, then balloons out from the elbow to the shoulder, where it is gathered or pleated into the bodice of the garment. Most fashionable in the Edwardian period, then again during the Edwardian revival period of the late 1960s and early 1970s. Also called a *gigot*.

mancheron: Worn by women in the mid-sixteenth century, a mancheron is a sleeve that is attached to the top of the shoulder then hangs loosely down the back of the arm.

melon sleeve, see *balloon sleeve*.

mousquetaire sleeve: a long fitted sleeve that for decorative purposes is shirred (i.e. gathered into two or more parallel rows) lengthwise from shoulder to wrist and softly draped.

oversleeve: a sleeve worn over another sleeve known as an *undersleeve*, sometimes held together by a collar piece. Often made of fur.

pagoda sleeve: a three-quarter-length or half-length sleeve style that is frilled to the elbow where it then widens into either several tiers of flounces or one large flounce seamed to curve in a shape that somewhat resembles a pagoda. The flounces are often decorated with bows or ribbons. Widely seen amongst upper-class women in the nineteenth century.

peasant sleeve: a long full sleeve set into a dropped shoulder and gathered into a band at the wrist.

puff sleeve: a short sleeve that is gathered into the shoulder segment of a garment to create a puffed effect. An eminently elegant creation.

push-up sleeve: a three-quarter-length or full-length sleeve with the fullness shirred to a band, with the result that when it is pushed up the arm it becomes a shorter, puffed sleeve.

raglan sleeve: a sleeve designed to allow the arms greater mobility, it extends from the neckline to the wrist, joined to the bodice by diagonal seams from the neck to under the arms. Named after Lord Raglan (1788–1855), British Commander during the Crimean War.

shoulder-puff sleeve: a long sleeve with a bit of a puff at the shoulder, but fitted from there to wrist. The predecessor of a sleeve with many puffs all along its length that was popular under the Tudors.

virago sleeve: an excessively full sleeve tied at intervals to form a number of puffs. Seventeenth century.

Five inspiring biographies

……………………………………………

- ☐ *The Invisible Woman: The Story of Nelly Ternan and Charles Dickens* by Claire Tomalin (Penguin, 1991)

- ☐ *Vivien: The Life of Vivien Leigh* by Alexander Walker (Orion, 1994)

- ☐ *Virginia Woolf* by Hermione Lee (Vintage, 1997)

- ☐ *Georgiana, Duchess of Devonshire* by Amanda Foreman (Flamingo, 1999)

- ☐ *Nora: A Biography of Nora Joyce* by Brenda Maddox (Penguin, 2000)

Pets

....

The three most popular names for pets are Max, Ben and Charlie. But to what kind of domestic companion should one ascribe this endearing moniker? Let the pets of the famous provide a guide (or warning) of sorts.

Pets of the famous

Odysseus (somewhere around 1200–1300 BC)	Argos	Dog	Probably the first dog ever written about. The relevant passage in Homer's *The Odyssey* has made many a grown-up weep, especially when read in the Robert Fitzgerald verse translation (The Fraulein Library, 1961).[1]
Isaac Newton (1643–1727)	Spitface	Cat	For whom Newton invented the first ever cat-flap.
Lord Byron (1788–1824)	Boatswain	Dog (Newfoundland)	Byron wrote a poem about him when he died.[2]
Elizabeth Barratt Browning (1806–1861)	Flush	Dog (King Charles Cavalier Spaniel)	Kidnapped a total of three times, a common occurrence at the time for London dogs of the genteel classes. Her owner wrote a poem about her.[3] Also one of the few dogs to boast her own biography: *Flush* by Virginia Woolf (Hogarth Press, 1933), written as a sort of memorial to Woolf's own spaniel, Pinka.
Charles Dickens (1812–1870)	Willamena	Cat	Willamena kept Dickens company in his study as he wrote, and when she wanted his attention she would snuff out his reading candle.
Florence Nightingale (1820–1910)	Athena	Owl	A fierce, expressive bird, Athena travelled in Nightingale's pocket and learnt how to bow and curtsey.
Leonard Woolf (1880–1969)	Mitz	Marmoset	Acquired in 1934. Mitz accompanied Leonard everywhere for a time, perching on his shoulder or inside his waistcoat. He even helped protect Woolf, who was Jewish, whilst on a visit to Germany with his wife Virginia in 1935.[4]
Paris Hilton (1981–)	Tinkerbell	Dog (chihuahua)	Born on Halloween 2002 in Athens, Greece.

Statistically, it is dogs who inspire the most literature (some great, some not-so-great) – marmosets and owls, not so much. These days, the choice of pets is wider than ever, sometimes overwhelmingly so. Tortoises are increasingly fashionable. To track one down, contact the Tortoise Trust (tortoisetrust.org / no phone / Tortoise Trust, BM Tortoise, London WC1N 3XX), which re-houses unwanted tortoises. Alternatively, as recommended by India Knight in the brilliant *The Shops* (the repository of a million fantastic shopping ideas), for a really low-maintenance pet, contact Insect Lore (insectlore.co.uk / 01908 563 338). They supply caterpillars, which can be observed in their hatching house as they develop into butterflies, at which point they are set free. They only last three to five weeks, so they are perfect for those with a low boredom threshold.

1   An extract from Book 17 of Homer's *The Odyssey* where Odysseus, disguised as a beggar, finally reaches his palace in Ithaka:

> While he spoke
> an old hound, lying near, pricked up his ears
> and lifted up his muzzle. This was Argos,
> trained as a puppy by Odysseus,
> but never taken on a hunt before
> his master sailed for Troy. The young men, afterwards,
> hunted wild goats with him, and hare, and deer,
> but he had grown old in his master's absence.
> Treated as rubbish now, he lay at last
> upon a mass of dung before the gates –
> manure of mules and cows, piled there until
> fieldhands could spread it on the king's estate.
> Abandoned there, and half destroyed by flies,
> old Argos lay.
>
> But when he knew he heard
> Odysseus' voice nearby, he did his best
> to wag his tail, nose down, with flattened ears,
> having no strength to move nearer his master.
> And the man looked away,
> wiping a salt tear from his cheek; but he
> hid this from Eumaios. Then he said:
> 'I marvel that they leave this hound to lie
> here on the dung pile;
> he would have been a fine dog, from the look of him,
> though I can't say as to his power and speed
> when he was young. You find the same good build
> in house dogs, table dogs landowners keep
> all for style.'
>
> And you replied, Eumaios:
>
> 'A hunter owned him – but the man is dead
> in some far place. If this old hound could show
> the form he had when Lord Odysseus left him,

going to Troy, you'd see him swift and strong.
He never shrank from any savage thing
he'd brought to bay in the deep woods; on the scent
no other dog kept up with him. Now misery
has him in leash. His owner died abroad,
and here the women slaves will take no care of him.
You know how servants are: without a master
they have no will to labour, or excel.
For Zeus who views the wide world takes away
half the manhood of a man, that day
he goes into captivity and slavery.'

Eumaios crossed the court and went straight forward
into the megaron among the suitors;
but death and darkness in that instant closed
the eyes of Argos, who had seen his master,
Odysseus, after twenty years.

2   'Epitaph to a Dog' by Lord Byron:

Near this Spot
are deposited the Remains of one
who possessed Beauty without Vanity,
Strength without Insolence,
Courage without Ferosity,
and all the Virtues of Man without his Vices.
This praise, which would be unmeaning Flattery
if inscribed over human Ashes,
is but a just tribute to the Memory of
BOATSWAIN, a DOG,
who was born at Newfoundland May 1803,
and died at Newstead Nov.r18th, 1808.

3   Extract from 'To Flush, My Dog' by Elizabeth Barrett Browning:

Loving friend, the gift of one
Who her own true faith has run
Through thy lower nature,
Be my benediction said
With my hand upon thy head,
Gentle fellow-creature!

Like a lady's ringlets brown,
Flow thy silken ears adown
Either side demurely
Of thy silver-suited breast
Shining out from all the rest
Of thy body purely.

4   From *Downhill All the Way* by Leonard Woolf (1967):
. . . for mile after mile the crowd shouted 'Heil Hitler!, Heil Hitler!' to Mitz and
gave her (and secondarily Virginia and me) the Hitler salute with the outstretched
arm . . . It was obvious to the most anti-Semitic stormtrooper that no one who had
on his shoulder such a 'dear little thing' could be a Jew.

Drink myths

There is a lot of guff talked about alcohol. The topic can turn perfectly intelligent individuals into credulous sots who are willing to believe anything and, invariably, in conversations about drink, fallacious scientific theories and superstitious balderdash go bizarrely unquestioned. It is always worth remembering that it is usually the person (generally, it must be said, a man) holding forth the loudest on the quality of the wine, or malt whisky, or whatever the drink may be, who is also spouting the most nonsense. Here are some common myths that should politely but firmly be put to rest:

Putting water in your whisky is sacrilege

In fact any distiller will tell you that adding water to whisky (up to around ⅓ water to ⅔ whisky) is an excellent way of opening out the flavours and aromas, and anyone who sneers at this practice is quite wrong to do so. Adding ice, however, will close down the whisky's flavour, and is a serve best reserved for the times when one would rather not taste the spirit in question . . .

Bits of cork in the wine mean it is corked

While it is undoubtedly tiresome if there are bits of cork in one's wine, it does not necessarily mean the wine is corked. The term 'corked' does not in fact refer to the cork itself but a substance known as TCA that is sometimes produced when chlorine solutions used to sterilise corks come into contact with mould in the cork. A wine that *is* corked will smell akin to a damp towel that has been at the bottom of the laundry basket for three weeks. A wine may also suffer from being oxidised, in which case it would smell stale, or from sulphur taint, when it would smell of rotten eggs or a struck match.

Wines with screwcaps, rather than corks, are naff

Screwcaps help prevent wine from becoming corked. As a result, a growing number of top-end winemakers now use screwcaps, *particularly* for their best wines.

Gin makes you sad

In fact, compared to most other spirits, gin is exceptionally low in 'congeners' – one of the main causes of hangovers – and is therefore far less likely to leave one sad and headachey in the morning.

A silver spoon in the top of the bottle keeps the fizz in champagne

This flies utterly in the face of all the laws of physics. The only way to slow down the loss of sparkle is either to stick a stopper in the top or to keep the bottle in the fridge, which slows the release of CO_2.

Older wine is better than younger wine

It depends entirely on the type of wine.

Beer gives one a beer belly, while spirits do not

Recent research suggests that a propensity for a beer belly is to be blamed on one's genes (in addition, possibly, to a weakening of resolve when in the chip shop at the end of an evening's imbibing).

Red wine for red meat, white wine for fish

Not necessarily. A light dry red may go perfectly with a fish dish, when a full-bodied, sweeter white would not. Consider the wine in the same way one would consider seasoning a dish – a grind of pepper, for example, may enhance both a steak and a bowl of strawberries. Above all, however, one must drink what one jolly well likes.

Useful phrases

	Please	Thank you	Hello	Would you like to dance?	Wow, you're gorgeous! Yes please, I'd love to.	No thank you. Please leave me alone.
Danish	Vær venlig	Tak	Davs	Vil du danse med mig?	Wow, du er gorgeous! Ja, behage, jeg ville elske hen til.	Ikke, tak for lån. Lad mig være i fred!
Dutch	Alsjeblieft	Dank je wel	Hallo	Heb je zin om te dansen?	Wouw, wat ben je mooi! Ja, graag. Dat lijkt me erg leuk.	Nee, dank je wel. Laat me alsjeblief met rust.
French	S'il vous plaît	Merci	Bonjour	Voudriez-vous danser avec moi?	Hou la, vous êtes splendides! Oui s'il vous plait, j'aimerais à danser.	Non, merci. Laissez-moi tranquille!
German	Bitte	Danke	Hallo	Möchten sie mit mir tanzen?	Wow, Sie sind wundervoll! Ja bitte, ja das wuerde ich sehr gerne.	Nein, danke Bitte lassen Sie mich in Ruhe!

	Please	Thank you	Hello	Would you like to dance?	Wow, you're gorgeous! Yes please, I'd love to.	No thank you. Please leave me alone.
Greek	Parakalo	Efharisto	Geia sas	Theleis na xorepsoume?	Wow, ise panemorfos. Ne, efharisto, tha eithela ply.	Oxi, efharisto. davs. Afisteme isihi, parakalo.
Italian	Per favore	Grazie	Ciao	Vuoi ballare con me?	Lei è magnifico! Sì per favore, amerei a.	No, grazie. Mi lasci in pace!
Portuguese	Por favor	Obrigado!	Alô!	Você quer dançar?	Wow, você é magnífico! Sim por favor, amaria a.	Não, obrigado. Deixa-me em paz!
Brazilian Portuguese	Por favor	Obrigado/a	Oi	Quer dançar comigo?	Nossa, você é lindo! Sim, adoraria.	Não, obrigado. Eu não quero nada com você, sai pra lá.
Russian	Pazhalsta	Spaseeba	Zdrastvooytye	Khateetye paytee patantsevat.	Ti preekrasna vigleedeesh. Da, pazhalsta, ya s oodavol' stveeyem.	Nyet, spaseeba! Astaf'tye meenya f pakoye pazhalsta.
Polish	Proszę	Dziękuję	Cześć	Czy chciałbyś zatańczyć?	O kurcze, jesteś boski! Pewnie, że chcę.	Nie dziękuję Proszę mnie zostawić w spokoju.
Spanish	Por favor	Gracias	Hola	¿Quisiera bailar conmigo?	Caramba! Estas muy lindo! Si, vamos.	No, gracias. ¡Déjeme en paz!
Swedish	Varsågod	Tack så mycket	Hej	Skulle du vilja dansa?	Wow, du är underbar! Ja tack! Jag vill gärna.	Nej tack, lämna mig ifred.
Chinese (Mandarin)	Ching	Shie-shie	Nee hao	Ni yao bu yao jen wo tiaowu?	Nee jen piao-liarng. Dwee, ching, wo yee-ding lai.	Boo-dwee, shie-shie. Ching nee dso ba.
Korean	Pootak-ham-needa	Kamsa-ham-needa	An-nyong haseyo	Choom-choo ro kaseege-ssumneekka?	Motjeem-needa. Ne, pootak-ham-needa, chaw-ssumneeda.	A-neeyo, kamsa-ham-needa. Hawa-ja eetge he-jooseep-seeaw.
Japanese	Kudasai	Arigato	Konnichiwa	Isshoni odorimasenka?	Sugoy. Hai, kudasai, zehi tomo.	Ie, kekko des, hitori shite oyte kudasai.

Useful phrases

	Please	Thank you	Hello	Would you like to dance?	Wow, you're gorgeous! Yes please, I'd love to.	No thank you. Please leave me alone.
Arabic	Min fadlak	Shukran	Ahlan	Hal tuhibb an tarqus?	Shaklak Hilw. Naahm, min fadlak. Sa-yusharrifnee.	Laa, shukran. Utruknee wahdee, lau samaht.
Hebrew	Bevakasha	Toda	Shalom	Ha'im tirtsi lircod iti?	Ata nie-e nifla. Ken, bevakasha, beratzon.	Lo, toda. Azov oti bevakasha.
Afrikaans	Asseblief	Dankie	Hallo	Sal jy met my dans?	Sjoe maar jy is oulik. Ja, dankie dit sal lekker wees.	Nee dankie los my uit.
Icelandic	Takk	Nei takk	Halló	Viltu dansa viþ mig?	Vá! þú ert yndisfagur! Já, þóknast, eg myndi gjarnan.	Neitun, þakka þú. Lattu mig i fridi.
Turkish	Mutlu etmek	Eyvallah	cehennem	Dans etmek ile beni?	Vay, sen are çok güzel! Evet, mutlu etmek, i almak senin davet.	Hayır, eyvallah. ayrılmak beni tek başına.

Cars

....

. . . are destroying the planet.

But for those who really must have one – for whom car-sharing or public transport are genuinely not viable options – then, pray, choose carefully. Buying a car is not just about how much money you can afford to spend: your car reveals more about you to other people than perhaps any other purchase you make, apart from shoes (and for men, wristwatches); hence deciding factors include not just the dull ones such as 'what colour?' or 'new or second-hand?'[1] (although these are important); far more crucial is, 'what sort of car best matches *me*?'

For the unimaginative, there are a plethora of creepily friendly Ford, Vauxhall, Mazda and Toyota dealerships that will offer you a delightful car with good fuel economy, metallic paint, a CD player, air-conditioning and go-faster stripes. If you absolutely insist on going down this route (if you need a practical, reliable everyday car for your family), then a vast array of monthly publications exist to

1   To which the answer is of course *always* second-hand. The moment you drive your 'new' car out of the dealership you are effectively losing 30 per cent of its value in an instant. And that can be a very expensive instant if you're driving out of a Mercedes, BMW or Bentley dealership.

help you with the decision. Among the best are *Top Gear* and *What Car?* They always have 'like-for-like' comparisons of cars within a particular class: sports cars under £20K, 'People Carriers', 'hot' hatchbacks, and so forth. Manufacturers update old models or launch new ones every year, so it is worth checking with these experts before you decide. Obviously an SUV of any kind is never, ever acceptable: it screams 'Hello, idiot approaching' louder than pretty much any other consumer decision you will ever make in your life. Mystifyingly, Kate Moss drives a Range Rover. Granted, for those who feel absolutely compelled to own an SUV, a Range Rover is the only brand that is even approaching the acceptable, but still. Boo hiss.

If you feel more adventurous (and you should), then looking further afield tends to prove infinitely more rewarding. The dreamers among us are often the first to consider 'classic' cars. These always look spectacular, but remember these cars are classics precisely because they were built *a long time ago;* therefore, forget extras like power steering, a decent stereo or climate control which would have seemed like impossible luxuries to the men (and they were men, not robotic arms) who built these cars. Furthermore, they tend not to be that reliable. It is never wise to rely on a classic car if you ever have to be somewhere at a certain time – for example, if you have a job.

So if you are happy to forego the Citroen DS, the Sunbeam Alpine, the MGB, the BMW 2002, the Triumph Herald, the TR7 *et al* (all decent enough in their own right but surely weekend cars and nothing more), then it would be preferable to seek out a car that is of a more modern vintage, yet manages to retain some sense of character. One example is the Jaguar XJ6. Redesigned in the 1990s with a 'retro' feel, this car is luxurious (acres of wood and leather), well-equipped (for the time), and yet will probably cost you less than a new Daihatsu Charade. Pete Doherty has a passion for them, and owns four, but heaven forbid that put you off. They are great cars and often well looked after by their golf-clubbing, gin-and-tonic-drinking former owners. For those under six feet with an eye for glamour, the Jaguar XJS is also worth considering – particularly the later 1994–6 models with the straight-6 engine.

For Jaguar, also read BMW and Mercedes. Both of these carmakers produce motor vehicles that last a very long time, yet whose high-end models have a similar rate of depreciation that is well worth taking advantage of: the Mercedes 500s of the late 1980s, the BMW 7 Series (an early 1990s model – technically sophisticated, mechanically sound) and the Mercedes E series of the mid-1990s are all excellent options.

Another make of car with character is the SAAB. SAAB was a fully Swedish company (and somewhat eccentric – they also build jet fighters for the Swedish air force) until the late 1990s when General Motors bought it and homogenised most of the styling right out of the design; but certainly the 900 series of the late 1980s and early 1990s is worth looking at, and not terribly expensive (even the convertibles). The Volvos of the early 1990s – the 240DL and the estate version of the same – are also cars that will run for a very long time, are easy and cheap to maintain and are available for not much money (despite now being film-makers' shorthand for 'these characters are cool' – Jarvis Cocker of the band Pulp famously drove a 240DL Estate). The new Mini (Madonna's vehicle of choice) should also be considered. While annoying the Mini purists with its distinctively 'non-Mini' size (when put side-by-side with most hatchbacks, the new Mini is pretty much the same size), the car does have the advantage of a unique retro look combined with contemporary engineering, which means it must be recommended – albeit only in one of the better colour schemes such as the gold, the silvery blue or the cream. And obviously never with a Union Jack roof. Good God.

Bear in mind that with many of the cars with larger engines, there is also the option of converting them to run them on bio-fuels (such as vegetable oil, the drawback to this being that the vehicle then smells like a chip van all the time) or LPG (liquid petroleum gas) – in which case you have the huge advantage of combining a good-looking car with the fact that you are destroying the planet at a marginally slower rate than at least most of the other drivers in front of you on the M6.

However, if a characterful car is less important to you than your children living longer than thirty-five years of age when the planet finally disappears under the rising waters of the oceans, a hybrid is the way forward. Sadly, none of the hybrid models currently available are particularly stylish or interesting (well, apart from possibly the much-lauded California 'sports' electric car, the Tesla Roadster, which also happens to be horribly expensive), but there is no doubt that the number of MPGs (miles per gallon) they are able to achieve does put petrol cars to shame. The Toyota Prius is popular among celebrities and available in several 'styles' – hatchback or saloon – both hideous. Honda make the Civic and Accord hybrids, along with the Insight. Lexus also offer an SUV hybrid and a luxury-class hybrid. All these cars are worth seriously considering for their environmentally beneficial impact; but, with most of the car industry now aware of the commercial success and mass appeal of hybrids, one can only hope that the next few years will bring hybrid cars with a bit more personality to match.

The alternative, of course, is simply to walk. The colourful and mysterious Edwardian playboy Harry Bensley dedicated seven years of his life to trying to walk all the way around the world with nothing but an iron mask and a pram full of postcards to assist him.[2] Who needs a car anyway?

2   The tale goes like this. One summer night in 1907, Harry Bensley was enjoying a raucous dinner at the Sporting Club in London with the fifth Earl of Lonsdale and J. P. Morgan, the most famous financier in the world. As the alcohol flowed and the room grew hazy with cigar smoke, a heated discussion erupted between this motley crue of moneymakers over whether, in a world of ever-shrinking frontiers, it would be possible to walk all the way around the globe without anyone finding out the walker's identity. In the heat of the moment, Morgan bet $100,000 (£21,000) on the fact that it wasn't. It was the largest sum of money ever gambled. Much to Morgan's surprise, even chagrin, Harry accepted the challenge. It was to change his life for ever.

Morgan attached strict and sometimes bizarre conditions to the bet. Harry had to pass through 169 towns around Britain, all in a set order, after which he was to embark upon a tour of 125 towns in eighteen countries all over the world, including Australia, Canada, Persia, Italy, Japan, Egypt, China and India. The trip was to be financed solely from the proceeds of postcards he sold en route. The postcards were to be stored in a pram that he had to push every step of the way. In an additional twist, he somehow had find himself a wife. And there was one last, crucial element to the expedition: to obscure his identity, Harry had to wear an iron mask – at all times. To this end, Morgan paid for a minder to accompany Harry to ensure that none of the conditions of the bet were broken.

On 1 January 1908, cheering crowds gathered in Trafalgar Square to wave Harry off on his great adventure. The few existing photographs reveal that he was an extraordinary sight to behold. Most memorable was the iron mask he wore – borrowed from a suit of armour owned by Lonsdale, it weighed over four-and-a-half pounds. Harry set off down Whitehall, pushing an enormous pram containing not a baby, but rather piles of postcards – of himself. His minder scuttled dutifully behind. It was the beginning of a long and eventful journey.

Over the next few years, the press brimmed with accounts of Harry's various exploits. At Newmarket races it was said he sold a postcard to Edward VII, though some claimed the King had asked Harry for his autograph in a cunning attempt to trick him into revealing his identity. In Kent, he was arrested for selling postcards without a licence, and later appeared in full regalia before the local magistrate. After a couple of years, such was the frenzy regarding his true identity that one newspaper offered a reward of £1000 to anyone who revealed it. An enterprising chambermaid attempted to win the money by hiding under Harry's bed – but, luckily, the minder discovered her in time. Perhaps it was because of the air of mystery that surrounded him that he received countless offers of marriage, many of them from amongst the most titled women in Europe. The iron mask apparently had its advantages.

Over the course of the next seven years, it is said that Harry reached Australia, Canada, the United States and possibly many other countries, and that he covered a distance of over 30,000 miles, all without ever removing his iron mask except to sleep. In August 1914, Harry reached Genoa in Italy. He had just six countries left to visit. But the arrival of a telegram at Harry's *pensione* brought devastating news – the outbreak of the First World War. J. P. Morgan allegedly offered Harry £4000 to settle the bet, a rather paltry sum by comparison, while other reports claim that Morgan called off the bet entirely as he was worried about the effect of the war on his financial empire. Either way, Harry had no choice but to return to England and enlist in the army.

An undefinitive selection of books published over the last five centuries

···

Just because a book is new does not mean it is any more worthy of our attention than many of the thousands of books published one hundred, two hundred or even five hundred years ago. Often, in fact, quite the opposite is true. With this in mind, below is a highly selective and un-authoritative list of notable, laudable or just downright eccentric books published over the past five centuries, all by authors who were British or at least based in Britain (a horribly parochial approach, of course, but one that brevity demands).

1507   *The Twa Mariit Women and the Wedo*[1]   William Dunbar

1607   *The Divils Charter*   Barnabe Barnes
*A tragaedie conteining the life and death of Pope
Alexander the Sixt. As it was laide before the Kings
Majestie upon Candlemasse night last by His
Majesties Servants.*

The Discription of a Maske   Thomas Campion
*Presented before the Kinges Majestie at Whitehall,
on Twelfth Night last, in honour of the Lord Hayes
and his Bride, Daughter and Heire.*

The Famous History of Sir Thomas Wyat.   Thomas Dekker
and John Webster
*With the coronation of Queen Mary, and the
coming in of King Philip, as it was plaied by the
Queens Majesties Servants.*

Jests to Make You Merie   Thomas Dekker and George Wilkins
*With the conjuring up of Cock Watt (the walking
spirit of Newgate) to tell tales. Unto which is
added, the miserie of a prison, and a prisoner. And
a paradox in praise of serjeants.*

The Englishmans Docter; or, *The Schoole of Salerne*
Sir John Harington
*Or, physicall observations for the perfect preserving
of the body of man in continuall health*

Triplici Nodo, Triplex Cuneus; or, *An Apologie for the
Oath of Allegiance*   King James I
*Against the two breves of Pope Paulus Quintus,
and the late letter of Cardinal Bellarmine to G.
Blackwel the arch-priest*

---

1   A poem in which 'the two married women and the widow' gossip about their differing experiences of marriage.

Volpone, or *The foxe*   Ben Jonson

Cavelarice; or, *The English Horseman*   Gervase Markham
Contayning all the arte of horsemanship

The Phoenix   Thomas Middleton[2]
As it hath been sundry times acted by the Children
of Paules, and presented before his Majestie

The Surveyors Dialogue   John Norden
Divided into five bookes: very profitable for all
men to peruse, that have to do with the revenues of
land, or the manurance, use, or occupation thyereof,
both lords and tenants: as also and especially
for such as indevor to be seene in the faculty of
surveying of mannors, lands, tenements, &c.

Pericles, Prince of Tyre   William Shakespeare

The Historie of Foure-Footed Beastes   Edward Topsell
Describing the true and lively figure of every beast,
with a discourse of their severall names, conditions,
kindes, virtues (both naturall and medicinall)
countries of their breed, their love and hate to
mankinde, and the wonderfull worke of God in
their creation . . .

1707   *Rosamund*   Joseph Addison
An opera, humbly inscrib'd to Her Grace the
Duchess of Marlborough

The Diverting Works of the Countess D'Anois
   Marie-Catherine, Comtesse d'Aulnoy
Containing (i) The memoirs of her own life (ii) All
her Spanish novels and histories (iii) Her letters (iv)
Tales of the fairies in three parts. Compleat. Newly
done into English.

The Practical Works of the Late Reverend and
Pious Mr Richard Baxter   Richard Baxter

The Platonick Lady   Susanna Centlivre
A comedy. As it is acted at the Queens Theatre in
the Hay-Market

The Lady's Pacquet of Letters   Delarivière Manley[3]
Taken from her by a French privateer in her passage
to Holland. Suppos'd to be written by several men
of quality. Brought over from St Malo's by an
English officer at the last exchange of prisoners

Arithmetica Universalis   Isaac Newton

2   Probably Thomas Middleton's earliest surviving play.
3   Britain's first female professional political writer.

A Poem Upon the Late Glorious Successes of Her Majesty's Arms   Nicholas Rowe

A Critical Essay upon the Faculties of the Mind   Jonathan Swift

Injur'd Love; or, *The Cruel Husband*   Nahum Tate[4]
A tragedy. Design'd to be acted at the Theatre Royall.

A Defence of the Rights of the Christian Church   Matthew Tindal

A Discourse Concerning a Guide in Controversies   Catherine Trotter
In two letters. Written to one of the Church of Rome, by a person lately converted from that communion

1807   *De Montfort*   Joanna Baillie
A tragedy, in five acts. As performed at the Theatre Royal, Drury Lane

Hours of Idleness   Lord Byron
A series of poems, original and translated

Memoirs of the Life of Mrs Elizabeth Carter, with a New Edition of Her Poems, Some of Which Have Never Appeared Before   Elizabeth Carter

The Libertine   Charlotte Dacre

The Peacock 'At Home'   Catharine Ann Dorset
A sequel to The butterfly's ball
Written by a lady

Faulkener   William Godwin
A tragedy: as it is performed at the Theatre Royal, Drury Lane

The Epics of the Ton; or, *The Glories of the Great World*   Lady Anne Hamilton
A poem

A Reply to the Essay on Population by Thomas Malthus   William Hazlitt

Phenomenology of Spirit   Georg Hegel

Critical essays on the Performers of the London Theatres   Leigh Hunt

Tales from Shakespeare   Charles Lamb and Mary Lamb

---

4   Poet Laureate 1692–1715, but best-known for publishing re-writes of Shakespeare like one of *King Lear* which features a happy ending and one of *Richard II* with all the characters' names changed. Tate also wrote the lyrics of the Christmas carol 'While Shepherds Watched their Flocks by Night'.

The Convict; or, Navy Lieutenant Eliza Parsons

Ellen; Heiress of the Castle Mary Pilkington

The Hungarian Brothers Anna Maria Porter

The Sportsman's Dictionary Henry James Pye
*Containing instructions for various methods to be
observed in riding, hunting, fowling, setting, fishing
Improved and enlarged*

Beachy Head, with Other Poems Charlotte Smith

Two Letters on the Subject of the Catholics Sydney Smith

Corinna; or, Italy Madame de Staël

Poems, in Two Volumes William Wordsworth

A Summer at Brighton Mary Julia Young
A modern novel

1907 *Recollections of a Humourist, Grave and Gay* Arthur William
à Beckett

Fraulein Schmidt and Mr Anstruther Elizabeth von Arnim

A Book of Caricatures Max Beerbohm

The Desert and the Sown Gertrude Bell

The City of Pleasures Arnold Bennett
A fantasia on modern themes

A Close Ring; or, Episodes in the Life of a French Family
Matilda Betham-Edwards

The Secret History of the English Occupation of Egypt
Wilfrid Seawen Blunt
Being a personal narrative of events

The Shuttle Frances Hodgson Burnett

The Secret Agent Joseph Conrad

The Lonely Lady of Grosvenor Square Mrs Henry de la Pasture

Through the Magic Door Arthur Conan Doyle

An English Girl Ford Madox Ford

The Longest Journey E. M. Forster

The Country House John Galsworthy

Three Weeks Elinor Glyn[5]

The American Scene Henry James

The Passing of the Third Floor Back, and Other Stories
Jerome K. Jerome

5 The bonkbuster to end all bonkbusters.

An undefinitive selection of books published over the last five centuries

Chamber Music   James Joyce[6]

The Furnace   Rose Macaulay

A Tarpaulin Muster   John Masefield

The Explorer   Somerset Maugham

The Enchanted Castle   Edith Nesbit

The Tangled Skein   Baroness Orczy

The Tale of Tom Kitten   Beatrix Potter

Bohemia in London   Arthur Ransome

The Life of Christ in Recent Research   William Sanday

John Bull's Other Island, and Major Barbara
   George Bernard Shaw

The Helpmate   May Sinclair

The Playboy of the Western World   J. M. Synge

Garibaldi's Defence of the Roman Republic 1848–9
   G. M. Trevelyan

Scapegoats of the Empire   George Witton

Not George Washington   P. G. Wodehouse

Deirdre   W. B. Yeats
Being volume five of Plays for an Irish Theatre

Ghetto Comedies   Israel Zangwill

6   *Chamber Music* was a collection of poems allegedly named after the sound of
someone peeing into a chamber pot, though in fact this was a tale Joyce fabricated
some time later. It was not a commercial success, with less than 250 copies sold in
the first year of publication, but the critics liked it. In a letter to his wonderful wife
Nora, Joyce confessed rather sweetly that 'When I wrote [*Chamber Music*], I was a
lonely boy, walking about by myself at night and thinking that one day a girl would
love me.'

An undefinitive selection of books published over the last five centuries

The ingredients of a Mac 'matte' lipstick

....

Octyldodecanol

Castor seed oil

Silica

Tricaprylyl Citrate

Ozokerite

Isononyl Isononanoate

Paraffin

Phenyl Trimethicone

Microcrystalline wax

Octyl Palmitate

Caprylic/Capriv Triglyceride

Carnauba wax

Ascorbyl Palmitate

Tocopherol

Vanillin

Stearyl Stearol Stearate

Britain's dependencies

....

Extraordinarily, Britain still clings on to no less than fourteen overseas dependencies. Governed by British laws, defended by British warships, taxed in British budgets, yet more often than not a thousand miles away – their perpetuation is distinctly peculiar:

Anguilla

British Antarctic Territory

Bermuda

British Indian Ocean Territory (including Diego Garcia)

British Virgin Islands

Cayman Islands

Falkland Islands

Gibraltar

Montserrat

St Helena, Ascension Island and Tristan da Cunha

Turk and Caicos Islands

Pitcairn Island

South Georgia and South Sandwich Islands

Sovereign Base Areas on Cyprus

NB: Britain is not the only nation that retains some leftovers of its empire. Baker Island in the Pacific is a Wildlife Refuge run by the US Department of the Interior but was inhabited up until 1942. The national day of Wallis and Futuna in the Pacific is Bastille day since technically it is still owned by France, while Norway continues to assert its rights to Bouvet Island in the South Atlantic.

Kate Moss

....

The object of a fashionable woman in dressing, is to make herself distinctive without becoming conspicuous – to excel by her union of graceful outline and fidelity to the fashion of the moment (no easy task), and, while offering no striking contrast to those around her, so to individualise herself that she is one of the few who remain in the memory, when the crowd of well-dressed women is recalled only as an indistinguishable mass. There are half a dozen women in London society who succeed in thus accomplishing a task that bristles with contradictions.

A description of Kate Moss? No, a passage from author Mrs Humphry's 1897 classic, *Manners for Women*, but one that is relevant today. Ms Moss is the one celebrity whom otherwise perfectly sensible, grown-up women seem happy to discuss for hours at a time. She is also one of the few able to inspire one to buy a product as a result of the advertising alone – why else would anyone over the age of fourteen ever buy Rimmel make-up? The fact is, she sends us all quite bonkers.

1991–1993
Mario Sorrenti

1994–1998
Johnny Depp

Careful analysis of Ms Moss's changing coiffure reveals a number of notable points. Her hair whilst she was with Mario Sorrenti was archetypally the hair of a young girl just starting out – natural, untreated and unteased. Similarly, it is no coincidence that she experimented a fair amount whilst with Johnny Depp, which was very much a rock 'n' roll phase for her.

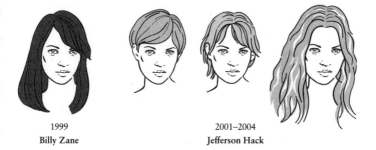

1999
Billy Zane

2001–2004
Jefferson Hack

Now in her thirties, her not-so-startlingly basic fallback position has become a long, very light brown, almost blonde, somewhat straggly look. All-natural in appearance, it is low maintenance and allows her to be a blank canvas of sorts for all the photographers who still clamour to immortalise her. Very sensibly, it seems to be a look that's for keeps.

2004
Daniel Craig

2005
Jamie Burke

2006–present
Pete Doherty

Kate Moss

Martinis

I love to drink Martinis,
Two at the very most.
After three I'm under the table,
After four I'm under my host.

— Dorothy Parker

In recent times, the term 'Martini' has come to mean anything strong, cold and in a Y-shaped glass; yet a truly authentic Martini should only ever be made from top-quality gin and/or vodka, with a little vermouth and possibly a dash of bitters.

Any aspirant Martini maker should take care to store their gin and vodka in the freezer at all times. To shake or to stir one's Martini remains a moot point. Some experts argue that shaking with ice 'bruises' the gin, and alters the flavour for the worse – if this is true, it does so on a scale undetectable to most human palates. What is certain, however, is that shaking does drive tiny air bubbles, and shards of ice, into the cocktail, making it slightly more dilute than one that is merely stirred with ice. In short, it is simply a matter of personal taste. Either way, the cocktail must be strained into a chilled glass preferably straight from the freezer compartment.

The art of the Martini lies in making infinitesimal changes with dramatic effect. Some variations on the classic recipe include:

- ***Traditional Dry Martini***: 2½ shots of gin or vodka and ¾ shot of extra dry vermouth, stirred with ice and the addition of a dash of orange bitters, served with olive or lemon twist
- ***Bradford Martini***: a Traditional, shaken rather than stirred
- ***Franklin Martini***: served with two olives, no bitters
- ***Dirty Martini***: served with a splash of olive brine and an olive, no bitters
- ***Gibson Martini***: served with two cocktail onions, no bitters
- ***Wet Martini***: heavy on the vermouth
- ***Vesper Martini***: 3 shots of gin, 1 shot of vodka and ½ a shot of vermouth and served with lemon twist, no bitters.

The truly sophisticated cocktail drinker confines herself to one of the above. The less ascetic palate may require the addition of fruit or liqueurs (and often the subtraction of vermouth), and many modern Martini recipes now pander to these tastes. There are as many Martini recipes as there are bartenders, but some more common ones include:

- ***Apple Martini***: vodka, apple juice and either apple schnapps or gomme (sugar syrup, which can be bought or made at home by dissolving 2 cups of sugar in 1 cup boiling water, reducing and then allowing to cool). *Approachable but somewhat dull.*

℣ **Espresso Martini**: vodka, cold espresso coffee, Kahlua coffee liqueur, gomme. *The alcoholic equivalent of class A drugs.*

℣ **English Martini**: rosemary muddled in bottom of a shaker, then stirred with gin, elderflower cordial and gomme. *Ladylike, and yet a suitably unusual choice.*

℣ **Chocolate Martini**: vodka, crème de cacao and extra dry vermouth. *To be consumed only in the company of friends.*

℣ **Lychee Martini**: vodka, lychee liqueur and lychee syrup. *Delicate and fragrant, possibly now a little 1990s.*

℣ **Lemon Martini**: lemon vodka, lemon juice, gomme, cointreau and orange bitters. *Stands or falls entirely on the quality of the lemon vodka.*

℣ **Martinez**: gin, sweet vermouth, cointreau, gomme and orange bitters. *Supposed to be the forerunner of the Martini, and excellent for creating an air of knowledgeability when ordering.*

The blues

Got the blues? At least have them in an unusual fashion – the Bremen blues, the Olympic blues or the Pompeian blues, perhaps. These colours have always existed, but it is only in recent years that paint manufacturers and computer programmers have bothered to invent a name for them. Let the lengthy list below shame you into allowing some colour other than black an outing to the office tomorrow.[1]

academy blue	azuline	bluebell
Adam blue	azure	bluebird
Airforce blue	azurine	bluet
air blue	baby blue	blunket
Alice blue	Berlin blue	bonny blue
amethyst	bice	Bordeaux blue
Antwerp blue	bloom	Botticelli blue
aqua	blue violet	Bremen blue

1 The alternative approach is simply to rebel, in the time-honoured tradition, against the rejection of black as one's colour of choice, this time employing as justification the manner in which Democritus (c.460–c.370 BC) viewed such frivolities: 'By convention there is colour, by convention sweetness, by convention bitterness, but in reality there are atoms and space'. (NB with atoms as we know them not yet discovered in the fourth century BC, in this context the word refers to a concept, co-invented by Democritus, which states that all matter is made up of a number of indivisible, imperishable elements.)

Brunswick blue
cadet blue
cæruleum
Cambridge blue
campanula
canard
celestine
cerulean
chambray
Charron blue
chasseur blue
China blue
ching
chinoline blue
chow
ciel
clair de lune
clematis
Cleopatra
cobalt blue
cobalt turquoise
Copenhagen blue
cornflower blue
Coventry blue
cyan
dark blue
dark cyan
dark slate blue
dark turquoise
deep sky blue
Delft blue
delphinium blue
Devonshire blue
Dodger blue
Dresden blue
duck-egg blue
empire blue
ensign
Eton blue
Flemish blue
forget-me-not blue
French blue
French navy
French ultramarine
garter blue
gentian
grobelin blue
German blue
grotto

grulla
heather
horizon blue
hyacinth blue
ice blue
imperial blue
Indanthrone blue
indigo
ink
international Klein blue
iris
Japan blue
Jersey blue
jockey club
kingfisher blue
King's blue
Labrador blue
lapidary blue
lapis lazuli
larkspur
lead blue
light blue
light sky blue
light steel blue
lime blue
Littler's blue
mackerel blue
Madonna blue
mallard blue
manganese blue
marine blue
matelot blue
Maya blue
Mazarine blue
medium aquamarine
medium blue
medium slate blue
midnight blue
Milori blue
mineral blue
mist
molybdenum blue
moros
National blue
Nattier blue
navy
nile blue
Nippon
Olympic blue

Oxford blue
pansy
Paris blue
patent blue
pavonazzeto
peacock blue
periwinkle
Persian blue
pervenche blue
petrol blue
plunket
poilu-blue
Pompeiian blue
powder blue
Prussian blue
Reckitt
Robin's egg blue
royal blue
Russian blue
Sanders blue
sapphire
saxe blue
Scotch blue
Sevres blue
sky blue
slate blue
smalt
steel blue
stone blue
telegraph blue
Thalo blue
Thénard's blue
turkin
Turnbull's blue
turquoise
twilight blue
Tyrian blue
ultramarine
venet
Venetian blue
vessey
Vienna blue
watchet
Wedgwood blue
woad
Yale blue
zenith blue
Zircon blue

The blues

Low spirits

....

'To: Lady Georgiana Morpeth.
Foston, Feb. 16th, 1820

Dear Lady Georgiana,

Nobody has suffered more from low spirits than I have
done — so I feel for you. 1st, Live as well as you dare. 2nd.
Go into the shower — bath with a small quantity of water
at a temperature low enough to give you a slight sensation
of cold, 75 or 80°. 3rd. Amusing books. 4th. Short views of
human life — not further than dinner or tea. 5th. Be as busy
as you can. 6th. See as much as you can of those friends who
respect and like you. 7th. And of those acquaintances who
amuse you. 8. Make no secret of low spirits to your friends,
but talk of them freely — they are always worse for dignified
concealment. 9th. Attend to the effects tea and coffee
produce upon you. 10th. Compare your lot with that of
other people. 11th. Don't expect too much from human life
— a sorry business at the best. 12th. Avoid poetry, dramatic
representations (except comedy), music, serious novels,
melancholy sentimental people, and everything likely to
excite feeling or emotion not ending in active benevolence.
13th. Do good, and endeavour to please everybody of
every degree. 14th. Be as much as you can in the open air
without fatigue. 15th. Make the room where you commonly
sit, gay and pleasant. 16th. Struggle by little and little
against idleness. 17th. Don't be too severe upon yourself or
underrate yourself but do yourself justice. 18th. Keep good
blazing fires. 19th. Be firm and constant in the exercise of
rational religion. 20th. Believe me, dear Lady Georgiana,

Your devoted servant,

Sydney Smith

Cardiopulmonary resuscitation

In 1767, the Dutch Humane Society issued the following guidelines for performing resuscitation: 'keep the victim warm, give mouth-to-mouth ventilation, and perform insufflation of smoke of burning tobacco into the rectum'. Alternative approaches prior to the twentieth century have included the victim being flogged, stuffed into a barrel and rolled down a hill, tied to a trotting horse, covered with hot ashes, and prayed for. Times have moved on, however, and now external chest compressions are generally thought to be the best option in situations of modern cardiopulmonary resuscitation, or CPR.

First summon medical help. Then double check that there really are no signs of breathing or a pulse. If there are not, ensure that the patient's airway is clear of vomit or other obstructions. Pinch the patient's nose, tilt the head back to open the airway, then cover his or her mouth with yours and blow out two long, slow breaths, one straight after the other.

If there is no reaction, follow this with chest compressions. With the heels of the hands placed on top of one another in a palm-to-back fashion and the fingers interlaced, find a spot directly in between the nipples in the middle of the chest just above the lower tip of the breastbone and use the heels of the hands to push down an inch or two relatively forcefully, afterwards lifting your hands back enough to allow the chest to recoil slightly, thirty times (it used to be fifteen but guidelines have recently changed) at a rate of a little faster than one a second or about one hundred a minute. Ensure that you are leaning forward a little so that your shoulders are over your hands; this will allow you to use the weight of your upper body to increase your strength, rather than tiring out your arms.

Repeat five times the cycle of two breaths to every thirty chest compressions, then check again for signs of breathings or a pulse. Continue this cycle until an effect is seen or help arrives. NB: This may take some time.

Then ask someone to make you a strong cup of tea.

Carbon emissions
(or, how to murder one's grandchildren)

Most climate models show that a doubling of pre-industrial levels of greenhouse gases is very likely to commit the Earth to a rise of between 2–5°C in global mean temperatures. This level of greenhouse gases will probably be reached between 2030 and 2060. A warming of 5°C on a global scale would be far outside the realm of human experience and comparable to the difference between temperatures during the last ice age and today.

If annual greenhouse emissions remained at the current level, concentrations would be more than treble pre-industrial levels by 2100, committing the world to 3–10°C warming, based on the latest climate projections.'

– The Stern Review, 2005

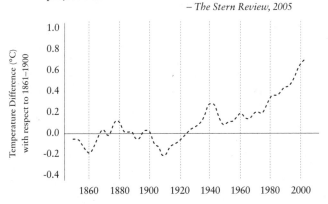

Signs of climate change are everywhere; nature is crying out for a detox. The details were recently laid out in *The Stern Review* by Sir Nicholas Stern (available to download for free from the website of the Treasury or in hard copy for £29.99 from Cambridge University Press). Evidently, the only way to help slow down the terrifying process of climate change is to reduce the amount of carbon that one's lifestyle generates. Yet it is clear from the table below that just one single aeroplane flight has the potential to cancel out completely all of one's admirable efforts to turn off the tap, to wear three jumpers rather than switch on the radiators or to use energy-saving light-bulbs (despite the fact they tend to emit a not-very-cosy fluorescent glow):

Destination	Distance travelled in kilometres	Carbon dioxide emissions in tonnes	Percentage of total annual allowance of carbon dioxide emissions used
Dublin, Ireland	898	0.1	5%
Barcelona, Spain	2368	0.4	20%
Stockholm, Sweden	2926	0.4	20%
Warsaw, Poland	2938	0.4	20%
Paphos, Cyprus	6418	0.7	35%
Nuuk, Greenland	6466	0.7	35%
Jerusalem, Israel	7242	0.8	40%
Teheran, Iran	8828	1.0	50%
New York, U.S.A.			
Almaty, Kazakhstan	11246	1.2	60%
Nassau, The Bahamas	13952	1.5	75%
Mumbai, India	14426	1.6	80%
Pyongyang, North Korea	17364	1.9	95%
San Jose, Costa Rica	17412	1.9	95%
Nanjing, China	17998	2.0	100%
Maputo, Mozambique	18382	2.0	100%
Manzini, Swaziland	18424	2.0	100%
Sao Paulo, Brazil	18974	2.1	105%
Buenos Aires, Argentina	22212	2.4	120%
Wellington, New Zealand	37660	4.1	205%

Figures have been calculated with reference to the *Stern Review* which suggests that, in the developed world, our carbon allowance, including both the primary carbon footprint (electricity, heating, etc.) and the secondary carbon footprint (food miles, share of public services, etc.), needs to be 2 tons per person per year (as opposed to the current figure of 9.6 tons per person per year) – that is, if human life as we know it is to have any hope at all of continuing into the next century.

Figures also assume that one is on a commercial airline on a direct return flight from Heathrow airport, rather than, say, a private jet, or a hand-glider, or for that matter a bird, a bee or Superman and therefore able to fly independently, in which case different rules apply.

Ideally, we should give up flying for fun. In real life, we won't – well, not for a while anyway – and so schemes have been developed to offset carbon emissions related to flying. British Airways, for example, now make it possible to buy carbon offsets: a return flight to Mumbai in India would additionally cost an offset payment of £12.22 (surprisingly little), which goes towards carbon reduction projects such as greener stoves for Indian schools with which to burn crop waste, rather than discarding it. Note, however, that these offset schemes are contentious: they may not fully compensate for the extra damage that CO_2 does to the high atmosphere, they are not always well monitored, and – above all – they help us sleep well at night when really we should be thinking about, and changing, our habits.

Carbon emissions

How to drive in snow

In extreme weather conditions, the best advice is: do not drive at all. If a journey is absolutely necessary, the following advice should be heeded:

1. Before setting out, ensure a full tank of petrol, tyres in good condition and a fully functioning car battery. Also pack basic survival equipment including water, food, a blanket, a torch, an ice scraper, some antifreeze and a spade. A mobile phone would be helpful too.
2. In icy conditions a car may require up to ten times the usual distance to stop – so adapt the distance between oneself and the car in front, and one's speed, accordingly.
3. Use headlights to increase the car's visibility to other motorists.
4. Use the highest gear possible to prevent wheelspin when pulling away, but when planning to corner, shift into a low gear and allow the car to slow naturally before applying the brake gently.
5. Be especially careful on bridges, overpasses and infrequently travelled roads, which freeze first.
6. If the car should start to skid, it is critical *not* to slam on the brakes, despite one's natural reaction to do so. Instead, take the foot off the accelerator and steer *into* the skid, before pumping the brakes gently (i.e. by resting the heel on the floor and pumping with the toes).
7. Should the car become trapped in snow, do not spin the vehicle's wheels as this will only dig it in deeper. Instead, snow should be cleared from around the wheels by a) turning them from side to side using the steering wheel, or b) using a shovel. Pouring sand, gravel, salt or cat litter in the path of the wheels may also help improve traction. Then accelerate away gently.

Ballet

The art of dancing has ever been acknowledged to be one of the most suitable and necessary arts for physical development and for affording the primary and most natural preparation for all bodily exercises, and, among others, those concerning the use of weapons, and consequently it is one of the most valuable and useful arts for nobles and others who have the honour to enter our presence not only in time of war in our armies, but even in time of peace in our ballets.

– *Louis XIV on the establishment in Paris of a Royal Academy of Music and Dance (1661).*

The term 'ballet' derives from the Latin verb *ballere*, meaning 'to dance'. Ballet originated in Italy during the Renaissance but was soon adopted with zest in France. From 1850 onwards, imperial Russia became the centre of the ballet world. This is reflected in the fact that today, three main methods are practised: French, Russian and Italian (also known as Cecchetti). The basic principles are the same, but some details differ.

The five positions of the feet

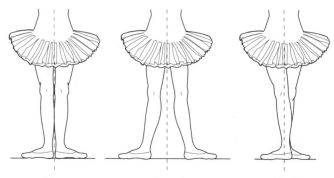

First   Second   Third

Fourth   Fifth

Commonly used ballet terms

arabesque: a position of the body, supported on one leg with the other leg extended behind and raised. Generally used to conclude a phrase of steps.

battement: a little like a beating action to watch, this is a step where the bent or extended leg is repeatedly raised then lowered.

cambré: arched, normally in relation to the shape of the body.

chassé: literally, chased. A step in which one foot chases the other out of its position.

ciseaux: a scissor-like movement of the legs achieved by opening both legs into second position, either while *en pointe* or in the air.

echappé: an 'escaping' movement – that is, when the feet are shifted from a closed to an open position, whilst remaining level.

en arrière: backwards. (Also *en avant*, forwards.)

en bas: low, or when the arms are in a low position. (Also *en haut*, high, or when the arms are in a high position.)

en manège: when the ballerina travels around the stage in a circular direction while performing her steps.

entrechat: a step where the ballerina leaps into the air and crosses the legs in front and behind each other in quick succession.

fondu(e): describes the action of lowering the body, usually by bending the knee of the supporting leg.

glissade: literally, glide. An action of the foot across the floor.

jeté: leaping from one leg to the other, with one leg thrown to the front, side or back into the air.

pas de chat: literally, a cat's step – that is, a leap of some kind, depending on which of the three different schools of ballet is being followed.

pas de deux: a dance featuring two people.

plié: a bending of the knee or knees.

relevé: a raising of the body on pointes or demi-pointes.

Ballets to note

The three most famous ballets in history are those composed by Tchaikovsky: *Swan Lake*, *The Nutcracker* and *Sleeping Beauty*.

Swan Lake

Swan Lake is based on an ancient German legend. Princess Odette has been turned into a swan by an evil magician, Rothbart. The only time she reverts to human form is at midnight. To break the spell, a man who has never been in love before must fall in love with her. Then along comes Prince Siegfried . . .

Swan Lake premiered at the Bolshoi Theatre in Moscow in 1877. The score required the full orchestral complement of strings, two flutes, two oboes, two clarinets, two bassoons, two trumpets, two cornets, three trombones, four French horns and a tuba, and – in the percussion section – a snare drum, a bass drum, a set of timpani drums, a triangle, a tambourine, symbols, castanets, a glockenspiel and a gong. Controversy immediately surrounded the coda of the *pas de deux* between the Prince and Odette in Act III. This consists of a sequence of thirty-two *fouettes en tournant* (turns on one leg), and it was the first time that so many *fouettes* had appeared in the context of a 'serious' ballet – which some saw as an amazing achievement, but others as sheer acrobatics. The feat is now a required element of every great ballerina's repertoire.

Sleeping Beauty

Inspired by the famous fairy tale, *Sleeping Beauty* is the story of the princess Aurora upon whom a spell is cast, which causes her to fall asleep for a hundred years. The only thing that can wake her is the kiss of a handsome prince . . .

Commissioned by the director of the Imperial Theatres, the first performance was in 1890 at the Mariinsky Theatre in St Petersburg. It was, however, something of a flop among both audiences and critics, and its genius went unrecognised until well after Tchaikovsky's death, sadly.

The Nutcracker

The Nutcracker is based on a German story called *The Nutcracker and the Mouse King* by E. T. A. Hoffmann. A young girl named Clara is given a nutcracker in the shape of a soldier for Christmas. She falls asleep, and when she wakes up, the nutcracker and all her other toys have suddenly come alive . . .

Premiered in 1892, again at the Mariinsky Theatre, the score is very much of the Romantic period in terms of style. Also notable is the innovative use of the celesta – a cross between a glockenspiel and a piano, it had been invented just three years earlier by the Parisian harmonium builder, Auguste Mustel. Tchaikovsky employs it most memorably in the 'Dance of the Sugar-Plum Fairy' in Act II.

One of the greatest versions ever of this ballet premiered in 1976 at the Kennedy Center in Washington, D. C. It was choreographed by and starred Mikhail Baryshnikov, arguably the world's greatest (and certainly the sexiest) living dancer.

The global AIDS epidemic

··

The estimated percentage of adults (aged 15–49) with HIV

Region/Country	Estimate
Sub-Saharan Africa	
Angola	3.7
Benin	1.8
Botswana	24.1
Burkina Faso	2.0
Burundi	3.3
Cameroon	5.4
Central African Republic	10.7
Chad	3.5
Comoros	<0.1
Congo	5.3
Côte d'Ivoire	7.1
Democratic Republic of Congo	3.2
Djibouti	3.1
Equatorial Guinea	3.2
Eritrea	2.4
Ethiopia	n/a
Gabon	7.9
Gambia	2.4
Ghana	2.3
Guinea	1.5
Guinea-Bissau	3.8
Kenya	6.1
Lesotho	23.2
Liberia	n/a
Madagascar	0.5
Malawi	14.1
Mali	1.7
Mauritania	0.7
Mauritius	0.6
Mozambique	16.1
Namibia	19.6
Niger	1.1
Nigeria	3.9
Rwanda	3.1
Senegal	0.9
Sierra Leone	1.6
Somalia	0.9
South Africa	18.8
Swaziland	33.4
Togo	3.2
Uganda	6.7
United Republic of Tanzania	6.5
Zambia	17.0
Zimbabwe	20.1
East Asia	
China	0.1
Democratic People's Republic of Korea	n/a
Japan	<0.1
Mongolia	<0.1
Republic of Korea	<0.1
Oceania	
Australia	0.1
Fiji	0.1
New Zealand	0.1
Papua New Guinea	1.8
South and South-East Asia	
Afghanistan	<0.1
Bangladesh	<0.1
Bhutan	<0.1
Brunei Darussalam	<0.1
Cambodia	1.6
India	0.9
Indonesia	0.1
Iran (Islamic Republic of)	0.2
Lao People's Democratic Republic	0.1
Malaysia	0.5
Maldives	n/a
Myanmar	1.3
Nepal	0.5
Pakistan	0.1
Philippines	<0.1
Singapore	0.3
Sri Lanka	<0.1
Thailand	1.4

Timor-Leste	n/a
Vietnam	0.5

Eastern Europe and Central Asia

Armenia	0.1
Azerbaijan	0.1
Belarus	0.3
Bosnia and Herzegovina	<0.1
Bulgaria	<0.1
Croatia	<0.1
Estonia	1.3
Georgia	0.2
Kazakhstan	0.1
Kyrgyzstan	0.1
Latvia	0.8
Lithuania	0.2
Republic of Moldova	1.1
Romania	<0.1
Russian Federation	1.1
Tajikistan	0.1
Turkmenistan	<0.1
Ukraine	1.4
Uzbekistan	0.2

Western and Central Europe

Albania	n/a
Austria	0.3
Belgium	0.3
Czech Republic	0.1
Denmark	0.2
Finland	0.1
France	0.4
Germany	0.1
Greece	0.2
Hungary	0.1
Iceland	0.2
Ireland	0.2
Italy	0.5
Luxembourg	0.2
Malta	0.1
Netherlands	0.2
Norway	0.1
Poland	0.1
Portugal	0.4
Serbia and Montenegro	0.2
Slovakia	<0.1
Slovenia	<0.1
Spain	0.6
Sweden	0.2

Switzerland	0.4
The former Yugoslav Republic of Macedonia	<0.1
United Kingdom of Great Britain and Northern Ireland	0.2

North Africa and Middle East

Algeria	0.1
Bahrain	n/a
Cyprus	n/a
Egypt	<0.1
Iraq	n/a
Israel	n/a
Jordan	n/a
Kuwait	n/a
Lebanon	0.1
Libyan Arab Jamahiriya	n/a
Morocco	0.1
Oman	n/a
Qatar	n/a
Saudi Arabia	n/a
Sudan	1.6
Syrian Arab Republic	n/a
Tunisia	0.1
Turkey	n/a
United Arab Emirates	n/a
Yemen	n/a

North America

Canada	0.3
United States of America	0.6

Caribbean

Bahamas	3.3
Barbados	1.5
Cuba	0.1
Dominican Republic	1.1
Haiti	3.8
Jamaica	1.5
Trinidad and Tobago	2.6

Latin America

Argentina	0.6
Belize	2.5
Bolivia	0.1
Brazil	0.5
Chile	0.3
Colombia	0.6

The global AIDS epidemic

Costa Rica	0.3	Nicaragua	0.2
Ecuador	0.3	Panama	0.9
El Salvador	0.9	Paraguay	0.4
Guatemala	0.9	Peru	0.6
Guyana	2.4	Suriname	1.9
Honduras	1.5	Uruguay	0.5
Mexico	0.3	Venezuela	0.7

*Source: 2006 Report on the global AIDS epidemic,
May 2006, U.N.A.I.D.S.*

How to eat a pineapple

....

'And as the race of pine-apples, so is the race of man'
– *William Makepeace Thackeray*, Pendennis, *1850*

For those who have not tasted a pineapple for a while, a revisit of this fabulously exotic fruit is highly recommended. Since the emergence in the 1990s of a new variety known as the Gold, they are more delicious than they once were – sweeter, less acidic and less fibrous – as well as more nutritious, containing over four times the previous level of Vitamin C.

Do not be deterred by the admittedly challenging task of ascertaining whether or not a particular specimen is ripe. Smell it, then ensure the leaves are green, the thorny 'eyes' are brown, and the base gives a little when squished. Bear in mind that the colour of the skin is the least reliable indicator.

To prepare a pineapple: first, slice off the crown and the base. Then, holding the fruit upright, slice the skin off in vertical sections all the way around. A few 'eyes' will be left – gouge these out with a knife (the tip of a potato peeler works even more efficiently). With the fruit still upright, slice it in half lengthways and in half again, then remove the core (this is actually the continuation of the fruit's stalk, which is why it is sometimes a little chewy).

The pineapple is originally from South America, and native tribes in Peru ate it chopped into small pieces and soaked in water and salt; in Colombia and Venezuela, it was boiled with manioc starch for breakfast, while the Caribs of Guadeloupe, which is where Christopher Columbus first stumbled across the fruit in 1493, used a mortar to pound the fruit into a thick paste, then seasoned it with capiscum peppers. The first official 'written' recipes featuring the fruit began to appear centuries later when the fruit reached England.

Five recipes featuring a pineapple

To make a Tart of the Ananas, or Pine-Apple. From Barbadoes. Take a Pine-Apple, and twist off its Crown: then pare it free from the Knots, and cut it in Slices about half an inch thick; then stew it with a little Canary Wine, or Madeira Wine, and some Sugar, till it is thoroughly hot, and it will distribute its Flavour to the Wine much better than any thing we can add to it. When it is as one would have it, take it from the Fire; and when it is cool, put it into a sweet Paste, with its Liquor, and bake it gently, a little while, and when it comes from the Oven, pour Cream over it (if you have it), and serve it either hot or cold.

– A recipe for a pineapple tart from The Country Housewife *by Richard Bradley (1732)*

Pare your pine-apples, and cut them in thin round slices. Weigh the slices, and to each pound allow a pound of loaf-sugar. Dissolve the sugar in a very small quantity of water, stir it, and set it over the fire in a preserving-kettle. Boil it ten minutes, skimming it well. Then put in it the pine-apple slices, and boil them till they are clear and soft, but not until they break. About half an hour (or perhaps less time) will suffice. Let them cool in a large dish or pan, before you put them in their jars, which you must do carefully, lest they break. Pour the syrup over them. Tie them up with brandy paper.

– A recipe for preserved pineapple from Seventy-five receipts for pastry, cakes and sweetmeats *by Eliza Leslie (1828)*

Ingredients – A small pineapple, a small wineglassful of brandy or liqueur, 2 oz. of sifted sugar; batter . . .

Mode – . . . Pare the pine with as little waste as possible, cut it into rather thin slices, and soak these slices in the above proportion of brandy or liqueur and pounded sugar for 4 hours; then make a batter . . . and, when this is ready, dip in the pieces of pine, and fry them in boiling lard from 5 to 8 minutes; turn them from the lard before the fire, dish them on a white d'oyley, strew over them sifted sugar, and serve quickly.

– A recipe for pineapple fritters from The Book of Household Management *by Mrs Beeton (1861)*

Preheat oven to 400 degrees. Then for each pound of canned baked beans, stir in 2 tbsp brown sugar, 1 tbsp syrup drained from Dole Pineapple slices, 1 tbsp catsup and 1 tbsp prepared mustard. Bake for 30 minutes, then top with drained Dole Pineapple slices and bake for 30 minutes more. Elegant enough to serve company – easy enough to fix just for the family!

– A recipe for canned pineapple with baked beans by the Dole Corporation's in-house home economist (1958)

Ingredients:
1 ripe pineapple
Demerara sugar, enough to fill a shallow dish
200g dark chocolate
125ml Malibu
2 tablespoons caster sugar (depending on the bitterness of the chocolate)
125ml double cream

Soak some bamboo skewers in water for 20 minutes.

Cut the top and bottom off the pineapple, and working vertically slice the skin off the fruit.

Cut into quarters and then into about three pieces again lengthways so that you have wedges of pineapple, cut off the woody core.

Thread the wedges on to the soaked bamboo skewers lengthways and lay in a shallow dish.

Put the chocolate broken up into pieces, into a thick-bottomed pan with the Malibu, sugar and cream and melt over a low heat. Then pour the sauce into dipping bowls.

Meanwhile, either grill or barbecue the pineapple, dredging it in Demerara sugar first, until it caramelises in the heat.

Dip the pineapple skewers into the hot chocolate sauce and eat.

> *– A recipe for caramelised pineapple with hot chocolate sauce from* Forever Summer *by Nigella Lawson (London, Chatto and Windus 2002). Bliss.*

How to eat a pineapple

The constellations

·······························

> Star light, star bright
> The first star I see tonight,
> I wish I may, I wish I might,
> Have the wish I wish tonight.
> – *Nineteenth-century nursery rhyme by Mother Goose*
> *(later borrowed by Madonna for her song 'Lucky Star')*

The arrangement of the stars has remained basically the same at least since written records began. A list compiled by the Greek astronomer Hipparchus in about 120 BC confirms this – the pattern is the same, as is the brightness, and they are even in almost the same place. Today the sky is (somewhat arbitrarily) divided into eighty-eight different groups of stars, each of which is known as a constellation. Especially significant are the constellations that lie along the ecliptic, which is the path the Sun appears to trace across the sky in the course of the earth's yearly cycle (in scientific terms, this is the plane defined by the earth's orbit around the Sun). These constellations are known as the signs of the zodiac. To identify a constellation, one must imagine lines drawn between each star – though, even then, few bear much resemblance to the mythical or semi-mythical beings after which most of them are named. Three of the easiest to spot from the Northern Hemisphere are:

Orion

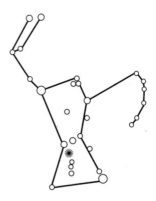

Visible from approximately October to March. Named after a giant hunter of Greek mythology. The key to finding him is to search the sky for his belt – three stars of similar brightness in a row in the middle of the constellation. Just below, look for his sword. Orion also contains a deep-sky object called the Orion Nebula(✹), which is a massive cloud of gases and dust where new stars are born.

Ursa Major

Latin for Great Bear, the
other name by which it
is commonly known. In
the Marshall Islands it
is called the Canoe, and
in Arab countries the
Funeral Bier (a frame
for carrying a coffin);
in Ancient Egypt it was
believed to depict
a thigh. Regardless, this
is the constellation that

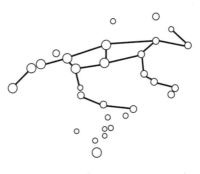

also features the famous Plough. Made up of seven main stars, the
Plough can be identified by looking north, then either just to the left
or the right.

Ursa Minor

Latin for Little Bear. At the very end of the bear's long tail, look for
Polaris, also known as the North Star or the Pole Star – located directly
above the North Pole. For centuries it has been used by travellers to
figure out which way is north (a fact to be borne in mind when on
one's way to a mini-break in the Hebrides). In Norse mythology, it is
the jewel on the end of a spike the gods stuck through the universe,
around which the sky revolves. It is 4,000 million million miles away
from the earth.

Of the other eighty-five
constellations, 32% are
named after inanimate
objects, 23% after land
animals, 16% after men
and women, 11% after
water creatures, 10% after
birds, 4% after mythical
creatures, 2% after insects,
1% after a geographical
feature and 1% after
someone's hair. An excellent
reminder of the important
things in life – compasses,
unicorns and air pumps
– they are also a rather
good source of out-of-the-
ordinary baby names.

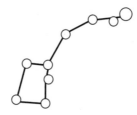

Name of constellation	Meaning	Name of constellation	Meaning
Andromeda	Chained maiden	Indus	Indian
Antlia	Air pump[1]	Lacerta	Lizard
Apus	Bird of paradise	Leo	Lion
Aquarius	Water bearer	Leo Minor	Lion cub
Aquila	Eagle	Lepus	Hare
Ara	Altar	Libra	Balance
Aries	Ram	Lupus	Wolf
Auriga	Charioteer	Lynx	Lynx
Boötes	Herdsmen	Lyra	Lyre
Caelum	Chisel	Mensa	Table mountain
Camelopardalis	Giraffe	Microscopium	Microscope
Cancer	Crab	Monoceros	Unicorn
Canes Venatici	Hunting dogs	Musca	Fly
Canis Major	Greater dog	Norma	Square
Canis Minor	Littler dog	Octans	Octant
Capricornus	Sea-goat	Ophiuchus	Serpent bearer
Carina	Keel	Pavo	Peacock
Cassiopeia	Queen	Pegasus	Flying horse
Centaurus	Centaur	Perseus	Hero
Cepheus	King	Phoenix	Phoenix
Cetus	Whale	Pictor	Painter
Chamaeleon	Chamelon	Pisces	Fishes
Circinus	Drawing compass	Piscis Austrinus	Southern fish
Columba	Dove	Puppis	Stern (of a ship)
Coma Berenices	Berenice's hair[2]	Pyxis	Sea compass
Corona Australis	Southern crown	Reticulum	Reticle[3]
Corona Borealis	Northern crown	Sagitta	Arrow
Corvus	Crow	Sagittarius	Archer
Crater	Cup	Scorpius	Scorpion
Crux	Cross	Sculptor	Sculptor
Cygnus	Swan	Scutum	Shield
Delphinus	Dolphin	Serpens	Serpent
Dorado	Goldfish	Sextans	Sextant
Draco	Dragon	Taurus	Bull
Equuleus	Little horse	Telescopium	Telescope
Eridanus	River	Triangulum	Triangle
Formax	Furnace	Triangulum Australe	Southern triangle
Gemini	Twins	Tucana	Toucan
Grus	Crane	Vela	Sail
Hercules	Hercules	Virgo	Maiden
Horologium	Clock	Volans	Flying fish
Hydra	Female water snake	Vulpecula	Fox
Hydrus	Male water snake		

All are best viewed on a clear, cold night, when one is dressed in a big coat and hat and gloves, and clutching a bottle of champagne in one hand and a lover in the other.

1 Named after an air pump invented by the British chemist and physicist Robert Boyle (1627–1691).
2 Named after Berenice (c.273–221 BC), the beautiful wife of the ancient Egyptian king Ptolemy III. She promised to sacrifice her long blonde hair to the goddess Aphrodite if her husband returned safely from battle. He did, so her hair was deposited in the temple. When it disappeared a few days later, the king was about to condemn the temple guards to death when the court astronomer declared that, in fact, Aphrodite had been so delighted with Berenice's present that she had placed it in the sky for everyone to admire for all eternity.
3 Named after the grid of fine lines in a telescope eyepiece that helps to centre and focus.

How to put up a tent in the dark

The most important step of all when putting up a tent in the dark is to remember to take the thing with you in the first place. Checking that one has the full complement of tent poles and pegs before one leaves is also advisable, otherwise it is not uncommon to be forced into one of two scenarios, both equally unsatisfactory:

a) bivouac in something like this

or

b) sleep with something like this

Indeed, it is advisable to practice putting up one's tent in the daylight, and somewhere dry, before beginning a camping trip, in order to avoid the pitfalls outlined below.

Figuring out which bit of a tent goes where has the potential to be infuriatingly confusing. As a result, many modern manufacturers now include a colour-coded system to help. But one will not be able to see this as it will be dark. It will also be raining, so it is essential to take plenty of bin bags to cover one's possessions and one's companions while they sit waiting on the wet grass.

Throughout the process, it is advisable to try not to lose one's temper, as even poles that have been designed for camping on Everest suddenly bend at right angles in the hands of an angry camper. Ditto tent pegs, if there are any left by this stage. If there are not, steal them from the tent next door.

It is important that the fly-sheet (that is, the second layer that goes on top) is kept taut and that it does not touch the main body of the tent, as this will alter the surface tension and cause a leak, followed by a kerfuffle. Securely pinned guy-ropes will help to maintain this structure; but they will also trip up drunken passers-by in the night, endangering the safety of the tent's inhabitants, so beware.

Some people try to make camping more fun by having a designer tent that is decorated with pictures of flowers or animals. This is a fruitless strategy, and is to be avoided, since dressing things up to be something other than they are is never advisable – not even when the tent in question is designed by Cath Kidston.

The most useful piece of advice when putting up a tent in the dark is to do it adorned in a gorgeous pair of Wellington boots. If decorated ridiculously enough, they have the wonderful effect of making even the most reluctant camper feel instantly twelve-years-old again. Ironically, Cath Kidston (cathkidston.co.uk) does a fabulous line in decorated wellies. Otherwise, try Harrods (harrods.com) for the best boots of this type, as well as for pet tigers.

Tattoos[1]

A practice originally known as 'pricking', tattooing only really became fashionable after 1862 when the Prince of Wales (the future Edward VII) was inspired by a visit to Jerusalem to have the image of the Jersusalem Cross tattooed on his arm. Early forms of tattooing employed combs, chisels or rakes to puncture the skin before adding the pigment. Some tribes in the Arctic used a needle threaded with soot-coated yarn. Methods have, however, moved on a little since then.

Tattoo location in relation to pain threshold:

HIGH PAIN THRESHOLD

Ankle (too painful due to proximity to bone)

Along the spine (ditto)

Neck (ditto)

Inside of the arm

Ribs

Hands

Feet

Outside of the arms

Shoulders

Back

LOW PAIN THRESHOLD

The tattoo machine as we know it was invented by an Irish-American named Samuel O'Reilly in 1891. It was based on an engraving machine invented some years earlier by Thomas Edison. The machine, the design of which has changed little since then, is a kind of drill, a bit like the one the dentist uses (the two sound identical, in fact). The drill uses a needle to puncture the skin by about a millimetre, thousands of times a minute. With each puncture, one drop of insoluble ink is injected into the dermis – the second layer of the skin after the epidermis, which is the outer layer.

Some describe the pain experienced when getting a tattoo as akin to the pain of a bee sting, pins and needles or being pinched. They are lying. Getting a tattoo is, after childbirth, among the single most painful experiences known to the human race. Indeed, many react in a similar way by screaming, crying, swearing or wishing it was over instantly. To this end, do not be over-ambitious in the choice of design.

1   Other words beginning with the letters 'tatt' include:
 • tatterdemalion (*adj* raggedly dressed and unkempt; *noun* somebody wearing ragged clothes)
 • tattersall (*noun* a pattern of squares or checks formed by dark lines on a light or brightly coloured background)
 • tatting (*noun* a form of lace made with a shuttle)
 • tattle (*verb* to gossip about other people's secrets)
 • tattler (*noun* somebody who gossips about other people's secrets; a long-legged shore bird that is related to the sandpipers and is noted for its loud cries)
 • tattletale grey (*adj* of a white colour with a grey tinge)
 • tatty (*adj* shabby, rundown or in poor condition)

The larger the design, the longer the pain endured. Also take a friend who is good at bullying you – or, even better, an acquaintance in front of whom you are reluctant to appear a coward. An ex-paramour also works well in this capacity.

Either way, it is imperative that the choice of location for the tattoo is dictated by one's personal-pain threshold. The closer it is to a bone, the thinner the skin and the closer the nerves are to the surface; therefore, the more it will hurt. It is not wise to take a preventative aspirin beforehand; this will simply thin the blood, with the result that one bleeds more and the process takes longer.

Other tattoo locations to be discouraged are: the breast (risk of sagging), the upper thigh (ditto), the stomach (ditto, as well as risk of stretching during pregnancy), and the face (obviously). In other words, any body part that is likely to change much in the course of a lifetime is to be avoided. Also bear in mind issues of visibility. How easy would it be to cover it up with a plaster at a job interview, Sunday lunch with the in-laws or tea with the Queen?

Even more crucial is the choice of design. For those keen to make a statement, entire body tattoos are becoming increasingly popular – sometimes with some plastic surgery to create a bifurcated tongue thrown in. For the less committed, try to dream up something that will retain its appeal even when you are 105 and spending your days drinking laudanum straight from the bottle. So, for a cellist, a drawing of a pair of F-holes on your lower back might be a suitable adornment, while those with a passion for tortoises or a penchant for apples could consider these as options. If your dream is to have the name of a loved-one tattooed on some part of you, ensure that in the event of a change of circumstances, it has the potential to be modified without too much trouble or trauma. The name Francesca, for instance, could in theory be adapted to read 'France', 'frantic', 'frank', or even 'frangible' (meaning 'capable of being broken or damaged'). This works better with some names than others. If your lover is a Ben, Dan or Sam, then go ahead, tattoo away; if he is a Sebastian, Muhammad or Reginald, caution is recommended.

Nobel Peace Prize winners

....

2006 – Muhammad Yunus, Grameen Bank
2005 – Mohamed ElBaradei, International Atomic Energy Agency,
2004 – Wangari Maathai[1] ♠
2003 – Shirin Ebadi[2] ♠

1 Born and based in Kenya, Maathai won for her contributions to democracy, human rights and, in particular, environmental conservation.
2 A lawyer from Iran, Ebadi has dedicated her life to fighting for the rights of women and children.

2002 – Jimmy Carter

2001 – Kofi Annan, United Nations

2000 – Kim Dae-jung

1999 – Médecins Sans Frontières

1998 – John Hume, David Trimble

1997 – Jody Williams[3] ♠ , International Campaign to Ban Landmines

1996 – Carlos Filipe Ximenes Belo, José Ramos-Horta

1995 – Joseph Rotblat, Pugwash Conferences on Science and World Affairs

1994 – Yasser Arafat, Shimon Peres, Yitzhak Rabin

1993 – Nelson Mandela, F. W. de Klerk

1992 – Rigoberta Menchú Tum[4] ♠

1991 – Aung San Suu Kyi[5] ♠

1990 – Mikhail Gorbachev

1989 – The fourteenth Dalai Lama

1988 – United Nations Peacekeeping Forces

1987 – Oscar Arias Sánchez

1986 – Elie Wiesel

1985 – International Physicians for the Prevention of Nuclear War

1984 – Desmond Tutu

1983 – Lech Walesa

1982 – Alva Myrdal[6] ♠ , Alfonso García Robles

1981 – Office of the United Nations High Commissioner for Refugees

1980 – Adolfo Pérez Esquivel

1979 – Mother Teresa[7] ♠

1978 – Anwar al-Sadat, Menachem Begin

1977 – Amnesty International

1976 – Betty Williams, Mairead Corrigan[8] ♠ ♠

1975 – Andrei Sakharov

1974 – Seán MacBride, Eisaku Sato

1973 – Henry Kissinger, Le Duc Tho

1972 – No prize awarded

1971 – Willy Brandt

1970 – Norman Borlaug

1969 – International Labour Organisation

1968 – René Cassin

1967 – No prize awarded

1966 – No prize awarded

1965 – United Nations Children's Fund

1964 – Martin Luther King

3 Awarded the prize for her work campaigning against landmines.

4 Born in Guatemala, Menchú won in recognition of her work promoting the rights of the indigenous people of Central America.

5 Won for her non-violent struggle to establish a democratic government in Burma (also known as Myanmar) which today is still governed by a military junta.

6 An advocate of disarmament.

7 Originally from Macedonia, Mother Teresa's work with the very poor, in particular in Calcutta, is well known.

8 Joint founders of the Northern Ireland Peace Movement.

Nobel Peace Prize winners

1963 – International Committee of the Red Cross, League of
Red Cross Societies

1962 – Linus Pauling

1961 – Dag Hammarskjöld

1960 – Albert Lutuli

1959 – Philip Noel-Baker

1958 – Georges Pire

1957 – Lester Bowles Pearson

1956 – No prize awarded

1955 – No prize awarded

1954 – Office of the United Nations High Commissioner for Refugees

1953 – George C. Marshall

1952 – Albert Schweitzer

1951 – Léon Jouhaux

1950 – Ralph Bunche

1949 – Lord Boyd Orr

1948 – No prize awarded

1947 – Friends Service Council, American Friends Service Committee

1946 – John R. Mott, Emily Greene Balch[9] ♀

1945 – Cordell Hull

1944 – International Committee of the Red Cross

1943 – No prize awarded

1942 – No prize awarded

1941 – No prize awarded

1940 – No prize awarded

1939 – No prize awarded

1938 – Nansen International Office for Refugees

1937 – Robert Cecil

1936 – Carlos Saavedra Lamas

1935 – Carl von Ossietzky

1934 – Arthur Henderson

1933 – Sir Norman Angell

1932 – No prize awarded

1931 – Jane Addams[10] ♀ , Nicholas Murray Butler

1930 – Nathan Söderblom

1929 – Frank B. Kellogg

1928 – No prize awarded

1927 – Ferdinand Buisson, Ludwig Quidde

1926 – Aristide Briand, Gustav Stresemann

1925 – Sir Austen Chamberlain, Charles G. Dawes

1924 – No prize awarded

1923 – No prize awarded

1922 – Fridtjof Nansen

1921 – Hjalmar Branting, Christian Lange

9 Won for her work with the Women's International League for Peace and Freedom, which she helped found.

10 Founder of the first settlement houses in the U.S.A. and President of the Women's International League for Peace and Freedom.

1920 – Léon Bourgeois
1919 – Woodrow Wilson
1918 – No prize awarded
1917 – International Committee of the Red Cross
1916 – No prize awarded
1915 – No prize awarded
1914 – No prize awarded
1913 – Henri La Fontaine
1912 – Elihu Root
1911 – Tobias Asser, Alfred Fried
1910 – Permanent International Peace Bureau
1909 – Auguste Beernaert, Paul Henri d'Estournelles de Constant
1908 – Klas Pontus Arnoldson, Fredrik Bajer
1907 – Ernesto Teodoro Moneta, Louis Renault
1906 – Theodore Roosevelt
1905 – Bertha von Suttner[11] ♀
1904 – Institute of International Law
1903 – Randal Cremer
1902 – Élie Ducommun, Albert Gobat
1901 – Henry Dunant, Frédéric Passy

Of the thirty-three women and 733 men who have won a Nobel Prize, the only ones to have been awarded it in two different categories are Marie Curie (Physics in 1903 and Chemistry in 1911) and Linus Carl Pauling (Chemistry in 1954 and Peace in 1962). This is not the only reason that Marie Curie (1867–1934) is to be forever worshiped and adored. See also page 20.

11 A radical pacifist and novelist from Austria.
   The first woman to win the award.

Seven variations of Morris dancing

....

Cotswold morris
Border morris
North West morris
Sword dancing
The Molly dance
Hoodening
Vessel cupping
Carnival morris (also known as Fluffy,
seemingly because it is predominantly
practised by women. Hmmm)

Shoes

....

> I think that when you get dressed in the morning, sometimes you're really making a decision about your behaviour for the day. Like if you put on flip-flops, you're saying: 'I hope I don't get chased today.' 'Be nice to people in sneakers.'
> – *Demetri Martin (American comedian, b.1973)*

A battle between high heels and kitten heels raged for some years but, thankfully, the latter have now been vanquished once and for all, relegated to their proper place as a late 1990s/early 2000s relic. The fatal flaw with the entire concept of kitten heels had always been that if a woman wanted to be comfortable, she might as well wear a lovely pair of flats. Why wobble around on a tiny spike that is only an inch high? If one is going to bother to wobble, wobble big, and ensure one's legs look longer in the process. Thus high – really high – heels have won their rightful place as the master adorner of women's feet.

High heels do present a number of practical problems to any woman who is not: a) a celebrity, b) a millionairess or c) any other kind of being who travels only in taxis, rather than one who takes the train or bus, or who trudges half a mile in the rain whilst trying to decipher a rain-splattered *A–Z*, like the rest of womankind; yet there is a solution. Wear high heels, but carry a pair of flip-flops in your handbag at all times. (In winter, replace flip-flops with fold-up trainers – try Rocket Dog, Adidas or Nike.) Simply change when near your destination. (The key is not to get caught mid-change, so embark upon the foot revamp not on the doorstep, but a couple of streets away at least.) Then one can run for a bus *and* sashay like Marilyn Monroe, all in the course of a single day. Hurrah.

Shoes are one of the few products where one does get what one pays for. This applies to high heels in particular – the more expensive they are, the more comfortable they are to walk in. As a result, they are one item upon which it is worth frittering away a fair bit of cash. To this end, try as often as possible to wear shoes to have adventures in, to paraphrase Vivienne Westwood.

How to walk for effect

1. Take small steps (hence pencil skirts give one a natural advantage because they force one to – Marilyn Monroe was no dumb blonde, it turns out).
2. Swing the hips.
3. Never, ever look back.

Shoes to have adventures in

Perfect for skipping down the boardwalk at Cannes.

Just right for a harvest festival. There is no danger of sinking into the grass in these, nor encountering any broken glass that may be strewn about.

These moc-croc trainers are destined for the final day of New York Fashion Week: in what other apparel can one expect to be able to race all over town, yet maintain the glamour that such a day demands?

Ugg boots are perfect for . . . nothing and nowhere. Worn for more than a day, one simply ends up with athlete's foot and a fatted calf – yours, not the farmer's.

Ideal when pregnant yet stubbornly refusing to look like a frump. Vintage shoes are an excellent way of picking up classic, high-end collectibles. All being well, they will not have moulded to the shape of their previous owner (who may have died. Wearing them. Such shoes are not for the squeamish).

Perfect for any event that does not actually involve standing up. This £10 job from New Look is only for the iron-footed: mostly crafted from a hard generation of plastic, it is a shoe that seems to be designed for something far more industrial than mere human feet.

Placing a bet at the horseraces

One night in 1783, the following bet was placed at Brooks's gentlemen's club on St. James's Street in London: 'Ld. Cholmondley has given two guineas to Ld. Derby, to receive 500 Gs. whenever his Lordship fucks a woman in a Balloon one thousand yards from the surface of the earth.' Since then, sadly, betting has become somewhat more tame in its focus.

The most common setting for betting these days is the horse races. This outdoor equestrian event is riddled with peril – one need only consult *My Fair Lady* (1964) or *Pretty Woman* (1990) to confirm this. Inappropriate attire, unseemly shouting and drinking too much in the Royal Enclosure are just a few of the potential sources of humiliation. Placing a bet, however, need not be one of them.

Places to bet

♦ *The Bookmakers*. Tend to be found in a ramshackle row shouting, making mysterious hand signals (a language known as 'tic-tac') and posting ever-changing odds on their respective (increasingly) digital) boards. Odds will vary from bookie to bookie, so select your man (and it almost always is a man) with care.

♦ *The Tote*. Rather less exciting than the bookmakers, the Tote kiosks are predominantly staffed by women in scarlet jackets, known in racing parlance as the 'ladies in red'. The main difference between the Tote and the bookmakers is that when one places a bet with the bookmakers, one is aware of the odds. This is not the case with The Tote, which pools all the bets and then uses this to pay the winnings.

♦ *Racecourse betting shop*. The same as a high-street bookmakers, and full of cigarette smoke, detritus, and depressed-looking men. Best avoided.

Odds

If one's horse should triumph, winnings are calculated on the basis of the horse's odds (also known as 'price'). If the odds are long, for example 50/1, the horse is unlikely to win; if they are short, for example 2/1, the horse stands a good chance of winning but, of course, one will win less if it does. Odds can be given in one of three ways:

♣ Even money (or 'evens'). This is when the bookmaker offers a return that is double the amount staked on a win bet – often displayed as 1/1. So if one's stake is £10, the win will be £20.

♣ Odds against. This is when the bookmaker offers a return that is more than double the amount staked for a win, i.e. if one's stake is £10, a winning bet at 2/1 (pronounced 'two to one' or 'two to one *against*') will return £20 plus the original stake of £10, making a total of £30.

♣ Odds on. This is when the bookmaker offers a return that is less than double the amount staked for a win bet, with the word 'on' indicating that the odds are reversed. A successful £10 bet at 1/2 (pronounced 'two to one *on*'), will return just £5 plus your stake, making a total of £15.

Types of bet

The types of bet one can place are numerous and can be dizzyingly complicated. Some of the more common types include:

🐎 *Win*. One's horse must win. The most straightforward and best choice for the beginner.

🐎 *Accumulator*. A bet involving more than one horse with the winnings from each selection going onto the next.

🐎 *Place*. One's horse must be placed second, third or fourth, depending on the race. A more flexible option, but one with lower returns.

🐎 *Each-way*. Essentially a bet combining a win and a place bet.

Picking a horse

The simplest way to study a horse's past form is to purchase a 'race card' on arrival at the racecourse – this is not in fact a card, but a booklet, which provides basic details on all the day's runners and riders. Factors to consider include: has the horse won before on a similar distance? What conditions has it performed best under? What is the going (i.e. the quality of the ground) like today? What kind of going does the horse prefer? Hard? Soft? Is the horse carrying significantly more or less weight than in previous races? Who is the jockey? Who is the trainer? Alternatively one can simply choose a horse with an auspicious-sounding name – the same name as one's pet rabbit or first boyfriend, perhaps. If still undecided, one should make one's way to the Parade Ring, where the horses are walked out before each race. This is an excellent opportunity to assess their fitness at close quarters. At the same time, one may also consider extra factors such as the jockeys' outfits (known as 'silks') – since as any woman knows, a pleasing colour scheme is of paramount importance to becoming a winner.

Once all these important decisions have been made, the money for the bet is handed over and one is given a ticket, which must be produced in order to collect any winnings. Bets can be made until moments before the race commences (though increasingly, they can also be made *during* the race – this is known as 'In Running' gambling). Bear in mind that, though impossible to explain in scientific terms, experience proves that the louder one cheers for one's horse, the more chance it has of winning. One final point: it is advisable to stay sober throughout. This, however, tends to prove rather trickier than it sounds.

Placing a bet at the horseraces

New Year's Eve

Only the peculiar or deluded actually enjoy New Year's Eve. The rest of us simply bear it as best we can. There is no doubt that it helps to be somewhere other than within a fifty mile radius of one's usual stomping ground, and ideally abroad – Paris, perhaps, or Brussels. This makes going to an over-priced pizza restaurant, elbowing one's way into a local bar, crashing the party of someone one doesn't know and trudging through the streets at 7 a.m. in search of a taxicab seem glamorous, rather than a nightmare. Alternatively, another excellent solution is to learn to play 'Auld Lang Syne' on an instrument of your choice, solving for ever the perennial problem of not having anyone to kiss when the bells strike midnight.

Music: traditional

Auld Lang Syne

Animal stings, bites or otherwise unfriendly approaches

With adventures come dangers – which should not put one off, but simply be borne in mind. When trouble of the animal variety arises, the optimum solution in most cases is to scream and shout, and seek professional help immediately. However, there are scenarios in which screaming and shouting will prove useless. So it is best to be prepared. Do not bother to look for Indiana Jones; he is never there when needed. *Be* Indiana Jones. Either way, an alligator attack is not to be tolerated – unless one is still carrying an alligator skin bag, in which case the poor creature has a point.

NB: Whatever happens, do not treat animal stings or bites lightly. If possible, seek qualified help. In particular, keep an eye out for signs of anaphylactic shock – wheezing, difficulty swallowing, a much-increased heart rate, swelling or itching anywhere other than the wound – because this can be fatal. At this point, professional medical attention definitely needs to be sought, and fast.

Bee or wasp

How to Avoid	Do not wear brightly coloured or patterned clothes that to a bee might look like a flower patch. In the case of both bees and wasps, if one does land, stand still. Do not frighten it. Do not make rapid movements. Blow on it gently to move it along. (See also page 28.)
What to do if attacked	Remove the sting with your fingers, trying not to spread the venom further under the skin as you do so. The pain will only increase if in the process you manage to puncture the bee sting's venomous sac. Remove it as quickly as possible because the venom continues to enter the skin up to sixty seconds after the initial sting. Wash the affected area with soap and water, then raise it to prevent swelling and cover with a cold flannel. Apply antihistamine if available to relieve the itching, then neck some painkillers.

Dog or cat

How to Avoid	Be kind.
What to do if attacked	Wash wound with soap and water. Elevate to above the level of the heart to inhibit swelling and avoid infection. Apply pressure with a clean dry cloth to stop bleeding. Then bandage. Should the bite occur in a country where rabies remains a possibility, it is vital that a vaccination be administered.

Portuguese man-of-war

How to Avoid — A large poisonous jellyfish found in the UK. Generally non-aggressive until disturbed. So keep an eye out for them.

What to do if attacked — Bathe the wound in vinegar – a trip to the local fish and chip shop is recommended to procure some. (See Page 10 for other uses for vinegar). Use Sellotape to remove any tentacles.

Spider or scorpion

How to Avoid — Avoid damp, dark areas, where spiders like to lurk. Check luggage because scorpions are famous for their stowaway antics.

What to do if attacked — Scrape off the stinger with a credit card or something similar. Apply ice for ten minutes, remove for ten minutes – this is to prevent tissue damage as a result of keeping the ice on too long – then repeat.

Jellyfish, coral or anemone

How to Avoid — Look out for them when swimming. All sting when disturbed.

What to do if attacked — Rinse the wound with salt water (not fresh water which will only intensify the pain). If stung by a jellyfish and the tentacles are still wrapped around the affected area, remove them, but be careful, wear gloves or use tweezers. Soak the wound for at least half an hour to neutralise the toxins in the tentacles. Anything acidic will work: urine is one option, but it does not contain enough acid to be particularly effective, so vinegar is preferable. Restrict the movement of the affected area to ensure the venom does not spread too much. Clean with disinfectant. Take painkillers.

Bedbug

How to Avoid — Move the bed well away from the wall. Leave a light on. Wash the bedsheets in hot water.

What to do if attacked — An antihistimine; painkiller pills; hydrocortisone cream: all will help relieve the horrid itching.

Stingray

How to Avoid — It hates to be surprised, and stings to scare you away. To avoid being stung, shuffle your feet along the seabed to warn any that are lurking that you're approaching – though be careful not to stub your toe, which can be pretty darned painful in itself.

Animal stings, bites or otherwise unfriendly approaches

What to do if attacked	Control any bleeding. Use clean, fresh water and some soap to clean the wound. The removal of the stingers causes severe bleeding, so ideally, leave the stinger until emergency care arrives. If care is not going to arrive for ages, remove any leftover parts of the stinger with tweezers. Never remove it from the chest or abdomen, though. Neutralise the toxin by immersing the wound in hot, fresh water.

Weever fish

How to Avoid	A small sand-coloured fish that buries itself in the sand on the seabed. In order to avoid, look out for the spines on its back. These contain venom so if you step on it, it will hurt considerably.
What to do if attacked	Remove the spines with tweezers. Wash the affected area, in the hottest water you can tolerate, for about half an hour – this helps destroy the venom.

Tick

How to Avoid	Wear long sleeves and trousers. Spray on repellent . . . blah blah blah – once the blighters decide they are going to cause trouble, there is little one can do about it except submit to the whim of these insidious pests.
What to do if attacked	Use tweezers to remove the tick – but use constant gentle pressure, otherwise you'll tear the creature in half and some will be left behind in the wound. Do not twist or jerk it out or try to burn it out. Examine the tick to ensure it has indeed all been removed. Disinfect.

Alligator

How to Avoid	Avoid lakes and rivers in tropical climes.
What to do if attacked	Run or swim away using whatever means possible; but if cornered, try to get on its back and push down on its neck to force the jaw down. Attack its eyes and nose with any weapon, even your fist. If it does manage to bite you, tap it on the nose. This often makes it open up its jaws again, which will allow you to escape. Go to hospital.

Lion

How to Avoid	Avoid the Gir Forest in north-west India and reserves and national parks south of the Sahara desert in Africa.

Animal stings, bites or otherwise unfriendly approaches

| **What to do if attacked** | Do not run. Talk to the lion in a calm but firm voice. Make yourself appear larger than you are – raise your arms or open your jacket out. Try to move backwards slowly, but do not turn your back on it. Do not make sudden movements. The aim is to convince the lion that you are not prey, but rather a danger. Fight back with rocks, sticks or anything available. |

Shark

| **How to Avoid** | Steer clear of the kinds of environments that attract a hungry shark – the mouth of a river after heavy rain; anywhere near a fishing boat; anywhere near where large groups of sea lions, seals, dolphins or fish congregate; anywhere near dead animals; anywhere near sewage, murky waters, the entrance to a harbour; anywhere you see fish or turtles behaving oddly. Do not wear orange or yellow or fancy jewellery which might look like fish scales. Do not splash about too much. |
| **What to do if attacked** | Get out of the water as quickly as possible. Control the bleeding by applying pressure on the wound. Remove any fragments of teeth or debris left in the wound. Keep warm. Do not move without good reason. Wash with soap and water and bandage. Go to hospital. |

Human

How to Avoid	Be kind.
What to do if attacked	Can be more dangerous than animal bites because the human mouth is even more of a hotbed of different types of viruses and bacteria.
	Apply pressure on the wound with a clean dry cloth to stop bleeding. Wash with soap and water, then apply disinfectant. Wrap some ice in a towel then apply it to the wound to relieve the pain (applying it directly might freeze the skin). Then bandage.[1]

1 Unless it is a love bite – in which case, ignore all the given advice, giggle, and congratulate yourself at still having the love life of a teenager. Then apply some toothpaste.

Animal stings, bites or otherwise unfriendly approaches

Major foreign-aid donors

....

	As a percentage of the Gross National Income	In millions of U.S. dollars
Norway	0.87	2 199
Denmark	0.85	2 037
Luxembourg	0.83	236
Sweden	0.78	2 722
Netherlands	0.73	4 204
Portugal	0.63	1 031
France	0.41	8 473
Switzerland	0.41	1 545
Belgium	0.41	1 463
Ireland	0.39	607
United Kingdom	0.36	7883
Finland	0.35	655
Germany	0.28	7 534
Canada	0.27	2 599
Australia	0.25	1 460
Spain	0.24	2 437
Austria	0.23	678
Greece	0.23	465
New Zealand	0.23	212
Japan	0.19	8 906
United States	0.17	19 705
Italy	0.15	2 462
Total	**0.26**	*79 512*

Source: Organisation for Economic Cooperation and Development Factbook 2006.

A selection of the world's largest cut diamonds

·······································

Golden Jubilee

Size	Shape	Colour	Location
545.67 carats[1]		Yellowish-brown	Thai crown jewels

Discovered in 1985 in the Premier mine in South Africa. Given to the King of Thailand, King Rama IX, in 1997 on the fiftieth anniversary of his coronation.

Cullinan I (also known as the Great Star of Africa)

Size	Shape	Colour	Location
530.20 carats		Colourless	British crown jewels

The Cullinan was originally the largest diamond ever found – 3106.75 carats. It was mined in South Africa in 1905 and named after the owner of the mine, Sir Thomas Cullinan. It was cut into a number of smaller pieces. Estimated to be worth about £200 million.

Incomparable

Size	Shape	Colour	Location
407.48 carats		Yellow	Diamond dealer in the US

Discovered in central Africa in the 1980s.

---

1 The carat derives its name from the seeds of a carob tree, which in Asia were once used to balance scales. Each seed uniformly weighed 200 milligrams and became the standard for measuring the weight of diamonds. So to convert a carat weight into grams, simply divide it by five – so, for example, the Golden Jubilee at 545.67 carats weighs about 109 grams.

Cullinan II

(also known as the Lesser Star of Africa)

Size	Shape	Colour	Location
317.40 carats		Colourless	British crown jewels

See Cullinan I above.

Great Mogul

Size	Shape	Colour	Location
280.00 carats		Colourless	Unknown

Discovered in India in 1650. Named after Shah Jehan who built the Taj Mahal.

Centenary

Size	Shape	Colour	Location
273.85 carats		Colourless	British crown jewels

The world's largest flawless diamond, found in South Africa in the same mine as the Cullinan I.

Great Table

Size	Shape	Colour	Location
250.00 carats		Pink	Unknown

Recorded in Golconda in south-central India in 1642; thereafter, it disappeared. The rumour is that it was re-cut and is now part of the crown jewels of Iran.

Jubilee

Size	Shape	Colour	Location
245.35 carats	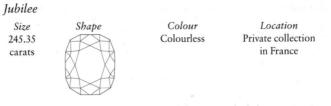	Colourless	Private collection in France

Mined in South Africa in 1895, in its rough form it weighed almost 651 carats; however, it was cut into its current form two years later, which was also the year of Queen Victoria's Diamond Jubilee, hence the name.

De Beers

Size	Shape	Colour	Location
234.50 carats	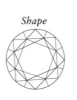	Yellow	Private collection in India

The first major discovery of the De Beers Corporation came from the Kimberly mines in South Africa. After its cutting, the De Beers diamond was unveiled at the Paris Exhibition of 1889.

Red Cross

Size	Shape	Colour	Location
205.00 carats		Yellow	Unknown

Put up for sale at Christie's in 1918, *The Times* described it as: 'Large and square-shaped, it has been cut with many facets and is of that pale canary yellow colour which is so sought after by Indian Princes. The play of the stone is very vivid. In artificial light it is much more luminous than a white stone. After exposure to brilliant light it emits the rays it has absorbed, and thus becomes self-luminous in the dark. Another rare feature is that a Maltese Cross is distinctly visible in the top facet. Hence the double appropriateness of its name, the Red Cross Diamond.'

A selection of the world's largest cut diamonds

For further information on diamonds, refer to Marilyn Monroe's stance on the matter, expressed in the song 'Diamonds Are a Girl's Best Friend' from the seminal and brilliant film *Gentlemen Prefer Blondes* (1953)[2]:

'The French were bred to die for love.
They delight in fighting duels.
But I prefer a man who lives,
And gives expensive jewels.
A kiss on the hand may be quite continental,
But diamonds are a girl's best friend.
A kiss may be grand, but it won't pay the rental
On your humble flat, or help you at the automat.
Men grow cold as girls grow old,
And we all lose our charms in the end.
But square-cut or pear-shaped,
These rocks don't lose their shape.
Diamonds are a girl's best friend.

Tiffany's! Cartier!
Black Star, Frost, Gorham!
Talk to me, Harry, Winston, tell me all about it!
There may come a time when a lass needs a lawyer,
But diamonds are a girl's best friend.
There may come a time when a hard-boiled employer
Thinks you're awful nice.
But get that ice or else no dice.
He's your guy when stocks are high,
But beware when they start to descend.
It's then that those louses go back to their spouses.
Diamonds are a girl's best friend.

I've heard of affairs that are strictly platonic;
But diamonds are a girl's best friend;
And I think affairs that you must keep liaisonic
Are better bets if little pets get big baguettes.
Time rolls on and youth is gone,
And you can't straighten up when you bend.
But stiff back or stiff knees,
You stand straight at Tiffany's.

Diamonds!
Diamonds!
I don't mean rhinestones.
But Diamonds
Are A Girl's Best Friend!'

(Music by Jules Styne, lyrics by Leo Robin)

2   Based on the equally seminal and brilliant book *Gentlemen Prefer Blondes* (1925) by Anita Loos, a feminist text well ahead of its time. The film version simply features lots of fancy frocks and a scene with Jane Russell in a gym surrounded by topless bodybuilders.

A selection of the world's largest cut diamonds

What to cook for a 'wild' dinner party

In 1940, *They Can't Ration These* by the Vicomte de Mauduit was published in response to the outbreak of war. A French aristocrat living in England, the Vicomte sought to reveal the pleasures of living off the nation's natural resources – its fields, woods, seashores and suchlike. The recipes he proposes also have the advantage that most of the ingredients are essentially free.

Nettle soup

Pick, wash and dry a pint glass worth of nettles. Scatter them into a saucepan containing a pint of water, then add some salt. Stir vigorously, then simmer for ten minutes. In a separate pan, melt an ounce of bacon fat, then add an ounce of flour, then the nettles and water. Cook slowly for another five minutes, stirring all the time. Add a smidgeon of hot milk, then a few croutons, and serve.

Roast hedgehog

Preparing the hedgehog is the mildly tricky bit. First, clean out the hedgehog's insides. Then roll it in some moist clay until it is generously coated and bake it in a moderately hot oven until the clay is dry and hard. Use a hammer to shatter the clay; when it comes off, the prickles and top skin of the hedgehog will stick to it. Finally, skin the legs. Then simply roast the remaining animal as you might a chicken, and serve.

Some other wild foods to look out for next time there is a dinner party to plan:

Samphire	Starling	Eel
Blackberry	Dandelion	Squirrel

What to cook for a slightly less 'wild' dinner party

A roast chicken is the perfect choice for any dinner party. It is incredibly easy to make, yet always looks terribly impressive, humans being the very visual creatures they are. Simply place the chicken in a roasting tray and smear it with butter, garlic, lemon (the juice, squeezed, and the rind, grated) and thyme – on its skin, up its bottom, wherever. The more the merrier, especially with the butter. Cook in an oven preheated to 200°C for about forty-five minutes for every kilogram of chicken, plus an extra twenty minutes for luck, basting it occasionally.

It is a truth universally acknowledged that one can never make too many roast potatoes. Boil the potatoes for five to ten minutes then drain them in a colander, shaking the colander vigorously in order to roughen up the outsides. Add to the roasting tray with the chicken and cook for about an hour, turning once, until crispy.

Finally, *jeux* the whole meal up with unusual or exotic vegetables such as red cabbage (the day before, ideally, fry an onion, then add a chopped red cabbage, a chopped cooking apple, two or three tablespoons of brown sugar and a liberal amount of cider vinegar, then simmer for a couple of hours) or sweet potatoes (roast them just like a potato but without the pre-boiling – sweet potatoes are less dense than normal potatoes, hence cook more quickly).

For pudding, see page 30.

Enough rules of football to get you through a season

Number of Players

Each of the two teams involved must consist of no more than eleven players, and no fewer than seven. One of these must be the goalie.[1]

When the Ball Is In and Out of Play

The ball is *out of play* when:

1. It has crossed the goal line or the touch line, either in the air or on the ground.
2. Play has been stopped by the referee.

At all other times the ball is *in play*, including when:

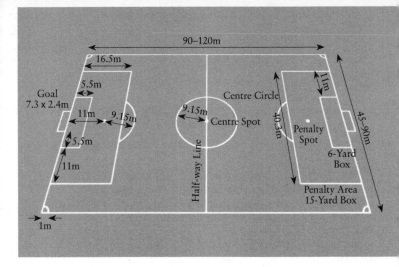

1. It bounces off the goalpost, the crossbar or a corner flagpost, as long as it remains within the field of play.
2. It bounces off the referee or one of the assistant referees, as long as they are on the field of play.

Scoring

The moment the entire ball goes over the goal line, beneath the crossbar and between the goalposts, it's a goal – as long as the team scoring the goal have not broken any of the rules of the game in the immediately preceding seconds, of course.

The Offside Rule[2]

A player is deemed offside if he or she is closer to the other team's goal line than both the ball *and* the second to last opponent. A player is not offside if he or she is level with the second to last opponent or with the last two opponents.

---

1   In terms of positions, traditionally, teams have played in a 4-4-2 formation – that is four defenders, four midfielders and two strikers. But that has changed in recent years and there are now a dizzying range of alternative options, as Sven Goran-Eriksson, the now ex-England manager, found to his cost in the 2006 World Cup, during which he used three different formations in the course of just five games – 4-4-2 twice, then 4-1-3-2 once, and then 4-5-1 twice – although the players he chose changed each time, so in fact no two line-ups were identical.

2   To be instantly considered a genius in certain circles, especially down the pub, memorise the offside rule word for word, and repeat at will.

Enough rules of football to get you through a season

Being in an offside position is not in itself an offence. A player is only penalised for it if, at the moment the ball is touched by a member of his team, he or she is involved in active play in one of the following three ways:

- Interfering with play.
- Interfering with a player on the opposite team.
- Gaining any kind of advantage by being offside.

Fouls and Misconduct

Direct Free Kick

A direct free kick is when a player is awarded a direct shot at goal. The taker of the kick is the only person who may score.

This kind of free kick is awarded if a player on the opposing team kicks, trips, jumps at, charges, strikes or pushes an opponent, or tries to, in a way that the referee deems to be careless, reckless or with excessive force.

It is also awarded if a player spits at or holds an opponent, tackles an opponent with the aim of gaining possession of the ball but makes contact with the opponent before making contact the ball, or deliberately touches the ball with his hands. The only exemption to the latter is the goalie – as long as he is within his own penalty area.

Penalty Kick

If any of the above offences are committed by a player within his own penalty area, regardless of where the ball is at the time, a penalty kick is awarded – provided the ball is in play.

Indirect Free Kick

An indirect free kick is when a player is awarded a shot at goal, but with the proviso that a goal may not be scored unless the ball is then touched by a player other than the taker of the kick before the ball goes over the goal line.

This kind of free kick is awarded if the goalkeeper on the opposing team, while inside his own penalty area, touches the ball with his hands after it has been deliberately kicked to him by a team-mate, after he has received it directly from a throw-in taken by a team-mate, or after it has been released from his possession and has not touched any other player, or if he keeps the ball in his hands for more than six seconds before releasing it from his possession.

It is also awarded if a player on the opposing team plays in a dangerous way, impedes the progress of a player, or in some way prevents the goalkeeper from releasing the ball from his hands. This is all subject to the interpretation of the referee, of course.

The Yellow Card

When a player receives a yellow card, it means that he or she is being cautioned. This happens when:

✗ A player is behaving in an unsporting manner.
✗ A player is showing dissent, either through his actions or his words.
✗ A player is persistently infringing the laws of the game.
✗ A player holds up the start or restart of play.
✗ A player does not respect the positioning required for a corner kick, a free kick or a throw-in.
✗ A player enters or leaves the pitch without the referee's permission.

The Red Card

When a player receives a red card, it means that he or she is being sent off the pitch for the entire remainder of the match. This happens when:

✗ A player is guilty of serious foul play.
✗ A player is guilty of violent conduct.
✗ Any player (apart from the goalie) deliberately touches the ball with his hands with the aim of preventing the other team from scoring a goal.
✗ A player employs offensive language or gestures.
✗ A player receives a second caution in the same match.

Homeopathy

There are an awful lot of people who are unaware of the wonders of homeopathy solely because of the persistent and absurd war between 'conventional' and 'unconventional' medicine. Homeopathy is a complementary medicine in every sense of the word. No respectable homeopath would eschew antibiotics if someone had pneumonia or deny someone a local anaesthetic if they were having a tooth out. But they would prescribe an immune-boosting remedy to work together with the antibiotic or offer a homeopathic gel to apply to the gum after the tooth is removed. People who use homeopathy have a tendency to be somewhat smug about it, due to the fact that they usually get better more quickly than those who deny themselves this extra help.

Homeopathic remedies consist of tiny white pills that taste slightly sweetish. One puts a pill in one's mouth, ideally straight from the container so that it does not react unduly with chemicals or germs on one's fingers. Try to keep the pill in the mouth for as long as possible while it dissolves – do not chew or swallow it. Caffeine and alcohol should be avoided whilst taking such remedies.

In a perfect world, we would all have our own homeopathic doctor who understands our constitution and prescribes remedies specifically for us. But failing this, buy a book and go for trial and error. It is often difficult to reach a definitive conclusion: for instance, if someone is bruised in an accident and is given Arnica (one every half an hour for two or three hours and then a couple a day), they might have got better anyway, mightn't they? Or, if someone feels sick and is given Nux Vom, the nausea might have disappeared regardless. This lack of proof means that some people discount homeopathy entirely; those who use it, however, know that it works. Though it might be all in the mind, of course . . .

Ten homeopathic remedies to try

- If one is bruised, either mentally or physically, take Arnica. This is the most amazing remedy, useful for any kind of physical exhaustion, accident, dental work, operation and even emotional trauma.
- For nausea or a tummy-upset, take Nux Vom.
- For cuts or sores, take Hypericum.
- For a cut that might get infected, use Calendula – it is the homeopathic antiseptic.
- If one feels the onset of flu, take Gelsemium or, even better, a little phial of a cocktail of homeopathic remedies called Oscillococcinum. Oscillococcinum is quite tricky to track down in the UK, but worth the effort – it zaps the flu before it has time to take over.
- For the first stages of a cold, take Aconite.
- For a cough, take Drosera.
- For muscle aches, take Rhus Tox.
- For period pains, take Magnesium Phosphate
- For a headache, take Byronia.

The origin of 'woman'

To ascertain the origin of the word *woman*, begin with the origins of the word *man*, with regards to which a variety of theories exist. *Man* may derive from the Latin word *manus* (hand), or from the Latin root *mens* (mind). It is more likely that it was inspired by a god known as Mannus who was worshipped by various ancient Germanic tribes. Whatever the truth, it is clear that *man* originally referred to a human being of either sex. In other words, our early ancestors were in no way trying to make some kind of sexist statement.

Man tended to function as a single syllable within a compound word. The Old English word for woman was *wifman*, where *wif* was a collective-plural noun meaning 'a family belonging to a woman' or 'womankind'. (In a similar construction, the Old English word for man was *wœpnedman*, where *wœpned* meant 'armed' or 'possessing weapons'.) The development of *wifman* into *woman* was then a slow, gradual process subject to a number of practical considerations – among them the fact that even once *wifman* had been shortened to *wuman*, this was found to be impractical in the context of medieval script where the letter 'w' was written as a double 'u'. The result was that 'wu' effectively appeared as a triple 'u', making the text not only tricky to read, but also in all likelihood raising (erroneous) concerns that the scribe had not been concentrating quite as closely as perhaps he should have been. Eventually the 'u' became an 'o' and *wuman* became *woman*. Elements of the word's etymology are evident today: the first syllable of the plural form of the word, *women*, has retained the pronunciation of the earlier form of the word, *wifman*, even though the singular form, *woman*, has stuck with the later one.

Similarly, the word *girl* has non-gender-specific origins and meant, simply, 'a child' – the root is *gir*, which is Scandinavian, with the final 'l' a diminutive suffix. *Lass* comes from 'rag'; *wench* from 'an unsteady one'; *queen* possibly from the Gothic word *quean*, meaning 'woman', though some sources relate it to the Old English word *cwene*, 'prostitute'.

Finally, let's delight in *daisy*, which derives from the Old English phrase *dœges eage*, meaning 'day's eye'. Is this because the flower resembles the sun? Because the petals close over the yellow 'eye' at night, only to open again once morning comes? Who knows. As Plato put it: 'The namegiver is the rarest of craftsmen.'

What to drink when

....

In the countryside: A pint of ale is a must (even if some of it ends up left in the glass to go warm). A hearty walk beforehand is the best way to work up a thirst for the joys of the local brew. It tends to be an acquired taste, but persevere, since every area has its own ales, each with different characteristics; one is sure to find one that suits eventually.

Girls' night out: Terribly out-moded until recently, rosé wine is now considered perfectly respectable, even chic. On the whole, the drier styles are far superior – the French and Portuguese tend to do these best. For the height of luxury, Krug Rosé Champagne is unsurpassed.

Alone in a bar: Not straight spirits, as this suggests a woman on the brink. For those who wish to be left alone, a glass of red wine is suitably neutral. In the post-smoking age one must confine one's attention to a good book. Failing that, nip round the corner to buy a newspaper (never resort to a mobile phone, which is simply gauche).

Hot date: Whisky never fails to impress. Scotch single malts are preferable – for extra cachet choose a peaty one from Islay (pronounced 'eye-lah'), as these are generally considered too challenging for female palates. But ensure you have the pronunciation correct before you order e.g. Bruichladdich ('brook-laddie'), Laphroaig ('lah-froig'), Bunnahabhain ('boo-na-ha-venn').

With the in-laws: Not a pint – in their day, women only drank pints if they were alcoholics or loose. Go for something suitably neutral like a gin and tonic instead.

In a fabulous bar: Be adventurous. If in doubt, ask the bartender to advise – they long to be asked, and may even provide a free tasting opportunity if business is slow. Fashionable spirits at present include gin, rum and tequila.

At Christmas: Mulled wine. Any excuse.

With the church choir: Sweet sherry.

With a Japanese businessmen: Scotch single malt whisky (it is incredibly expensive in Japan).

In a Spanish finca at about 6.30 p.m. in July: Cold, dry sherry.

On reaching the North Pole: Zubrowka bison grass vodka mixed with apple juice. A vastly under-rated drink.

In a time machine on the way to nineteenth-century Paris accompanied by Toulouse-Lautrec and three prostitutes: Absinthe. In no other circumstances is this an acceptable tipple.

Therapy

Contrary to popular belief, therapy does actually work – it is not just for Americans and/or psychopaths. If it is considered reasonable to pay someone to clean your house, then why not your head? The key is simply not to do it for ever. There are many different types of therapy, all of which can, in essence, be traced back to the work of Sigmund Freud (1856–1939).

Types of therapy

Psychodynamic

By 1896, Freud had developed a method of working with neurotic Victorian women that he called 'psychoanalysis'. It involved making them lie on a couch and talk to him about what was going on in their over-emotional heads. His approach focused on the dynamics of the relationship between the psyche and the external world. The resulting 'psychodynamic' therapies concentrate on the feelings (often unconscious, according to Freud) we have about ourselves or other people.

Psychodynamic treatment involves harping on about past experiences, endlessly surmising how these may have led to one's present situation, and why The Past may now be ruining one's life. The therapist tends to say little, other than to make various opaque 'interpretations' of the client's statements. Any understanding gained from psychodynamic discussion allegedly frees the client from the future repetition of destructive patterns. If one's problems are long-standing, treatment may last a good many expensive months, even years. Woody Allen, after spending forty years on the couch, eventually admitted that he thought the process irrelevant – despite once consulting his shrink on the decision to make the switch from polyester sheets to cotton ones.

Humanistic

In the 1940s and 1950s, American psychologist Carl Rogers developed his own ideas in response to Freud's psychodynamic ones. Now known as 'humanistic' therapy, Rogers's 'nice' therapy places significant emphasis on recognising human capabilities in areas such as personal choice, creativity and development (thus making it more of an artistic rather than scientific approach). It also focuses on the therapist holding 'unconditional positive regard' for the client – in other words, the client is always right and the therapist's opinion is of no importance. Hence, this 'client-centred' humanistic therapy can easily let one off the hook, with the therapist saying things like 'I can see that makes you feel sad' a lot, and always taking the client's side.

However, from the 1960s onwards the humanistic movement branched out into increasingly 'relationship-centred' types of therapy – among them Gestalt, Existential and Transactional Analysis. These focus on a more equal relationship between the client and the therapist in which the therapist gives (often highly challenging) feedback in order to help individuals recognise their own strengths.

Behavioural

Modern behavioural therapy first emerged in the 1950s and evolved under the influence of theories of how people learn. Rejecting the notion of 'hidden' aspects of the mind, which cannot be proven to exist, practitioners in the behavioural tradition began to focus on what could actually be observed in the outside world. Behavioural methods attempt to change patterns of behaviour more directly. These methods can be fairly brutal: patients are often forced to overcome their fears by spending increasing amounts of time in the situation they dread or being made to endure various anxiety-provoking experiences. Patients are given 'homework' and have to keep diaries and practise new skills between sessions. Behavioural therapies are thought to be effective for all manner of issues, ranging from anxiety to obsessive-compulsive disorders to sexual difficulties. Relief from symptoms often occurs quite quickly, which is why this approach is seen as a bargain, compared to the financial drain of the other, talking cures.

Cognitive Behavioural Therapy, however, combines both. Rather than focusing on the past, it aims at changing thinking patterns directly and encourages discussion to help rid oneself of silly thinking. It is currently being lauded as *the* new cure for depression.

Family/Marital

There comes a time in everyone's life when one finally has to realise that not *all* of one's problems can be blamed on other people – husbands, mothers or more popular siblings, for example. To this end, family or marital therapy, which began in the 1960s and was born of a technical and philosophical departure from traditional individual treatment, advocates everyone sitting down – together – to have a good chat. Squirming, all the participants put their side across. The therapist then attempts to dodge the flying furniture, and focus objectively on what is really going on.

A GP can make referrals to a qualified psychotherapist; otherwise, word-of-mouth is the best recommendation, so be brave and ask around. The therapist must have a *recognised* (and not just by themselves) qualification. Do not be afraid to shop about for someone who suits: one would not dream of buying the first winter coat one tried on, after all.

The thank-you letter

....

When to write a thank-you letter

Always.

(For the single exception to this rule, see page 25.)

The concept of a 'thank-you letter' is actually a misnomer. A letter suggests someone with too much time on her hands – unless, obviously, it is in response to an amazingly spectacular present or an entire week away. In almost all other cases, a simple postcard will suffice. Make a point of picking up suitable postcards wherever you go – it is eminently satisfying to be able to match the postcard to the recipient in a witty or wise way. For inspiration for the composition of such missives, refer to the two examples below: one from Samuel Johnson thanking Lord Bute for a royal pension that is rather courtly and conventional in style, followed by one from Lord Byron to his publisher John Murray which is very dismissive of a present of books, but so well written that it all but makes up for the insult.

20 July, 1762.

My Lord,

When the bills were yesterday delivered to me by Mr Wedderburne, I was informed by him of the future favours which His Majesty has by your Lordship's recommendation been induced to intend for me.

Bounty always receives part of its value from the manner in which it is bestowed; your Lordship's kindness includes every circumstance that can gratify delicacy, or enforce obligation. You have conferred your favours on a Man who has neither alliance nor interest, who has nor merited them by services, nor courted them by officiousness; you have spared him the shame of solicitation, and the anxiety of suspense.

What has been thus elegantly given, will, I hope, not be reproachfully enjoyed; I shall endeavour to give your Lordship the only recompense, which generosity desires, the gratification of finding that your benefits are not improperly bestowed. I am, My Lord, Your Lordship's most obliged, most obedient, and most humble servant,

Sam. Johnson

12 September, 1821.

Dear Sir,

. . . I have no patience with the sort of trash you send me out by way of books; except Scott's novels, and three or four other things, I never saw such work or works. Campbell is lecturing – Moore idling – Southey twaddling – Wordsworth driveling – Coleridge muddling – Joanna Baillie piddling – Bowles quibbling, squabbling, and sniveling.

Yours,

Byron.

Forms of address

Debrett's prescribes the following for the trickier-named members of society:[1]

Name	Envelope	Beginning of a Letter	Verbal Address	Place Card
Duke	The Duke of Northangerland	Dear Duke or Dear Duke of Northangerland	Duke	Duke of Northangerland
Duchess	The Duchess of Northangerland	Dear Duchess or Dear Duchess of Northangerland	Duchess	Duchess of Northangerland
Daughter of a duke	The Lady Mary Percy	Dear Lady Mary	Lady Mary	Lady Mary Percy
Eldest son of a duke	Marquess of Douro	Dear Lord Douro	Lord Douro	Lord Douro
Younger son of a duke	The Lord Alexander Percy	Dear Lord Alexander	Lord Alexander	Lord Alexander Percy
Earl	The Earl of Alnwick	Dear Lord Alnwick	Lord Alnwick	Lord Alnwick
Countess	The Countess of Alnwick	Dear Lady Alnwick	Lady Alnwick	Lady Alnwick
Daughter of an earl	The Lady Louisa Dance	Dear Lady Louisa	Lady Louisa	Lady Louisa Dance
Eldest son of an earl	Viscount Verreopolis	Dear Lord Verreopolis	Lord Verreopolis	Lord Verreopolis
Younger son of an earl	The Hon. Luke Dance	Dear Mr Dance	Mr Dance	Mr Luke Dance
Life peer	The Lord Townsend of Glasstown	Dear Lord Townsend	Lord Townsend	Lord Townsend
Wife of life peer	The Lady Townsend of Glasstown	Dear Lady Townsend	Lady Townsend	Lady Townsend
Children of life peer	The Hon. Charles Townsend	Dear Mr Townsend	Mr Townsend	Mr Charles Townsend
Knight	Sir John Flower	Dear Sir John	Sir John	Sir John Flower
Knight's wife	Lady Flower	Dear Lady Flower	Lady Flower	Lady Flower
Hereditary peeress in her own right	The Countess of Zamorna	Dear Lady Zamorna	Lady Zamorna	Lady Zamorna
Widow of hereditary peer	Mary, Duchess of Zamorna	Dear Lady Zamorna	Lady Zamorna	Lady Zamorna

1 The names used to demonstrate the correct forms of address are plundered from the fictional world of Angria that was invented by Charlotte, Branwell, Emily and Anne Brontë when they were children. A number of liberties have been taken.

The thank-you letter

Name	Envelope	Beginning of a Letter	Verbal Address	Place Card
Former wife of hereditary peer	Mary, Countess of Zamorna	Dear Lady Zamorna	Lady Zamorna	Lady Zamorna
Life peeress	The Baroness Percy of Verdopolis	Dear Lady Percy	Lady Percy	Lady Percy
Dame	Dame Mary Percy	Dear Dame Mary	Dame Mary	Dame Mary Percy
Scottish chieftain (female)	Madam/Mrs MacHart of MacHart	Dear Madam/Mrs MacHart of MacHart	Madam/Mrs MacHart of MacHart	Madam/Mrs MacHart of MacHart
Scottish chieftain (male)	The MacHart of MacHart	Dear MacHart of MacHart	MacHart of MacHart	The MacHart of MacHart
Wife of Scottish chieftain	Madam or Mrs MacDance of MacDance	Dear Dear Madam/Mrs MacHart of MacHart	Madam/Mrs MacHart of MacHart	Madam/Mrs MacHart of MacHart
Irish chieftain	The O'Rogue of the Roguetown	Dear O'Rogue	O'Rogue	The O'Rogue of the Roguetown
Wife of Irish chieftain	Madam O'Rogue of the Roguetown	Dear Madam O'Rogue	Madam O'Rogue	Madam O'Rogue of the Roguetown
Prime Minister	The Rt. Hon. Young Soult MP, The Prime Minister	Dear Prime Minister	Prime Minister	Prime Minister
High court judge (female)	The Hon. Ms/Miss/Mrs Justice Hume	Dear Judge/Dear Dame Marian	Dame Marian	Mrs Justice Hume
High court judge (male)	The Hon. Mr Justice Rhymer	Dear Lord Justice	Lord Justice	Lord Justice Rhymer
Admiral of the Fleet	Admiral of the Fleet, the Earl of Ellrington	Dear Lord Ellrington	Lord Ellrington	Admiral of the Fleet Lord Ellrington
The Chief Rabbi	The Chief Rabbi	Dear Chief Rabbi	Chief Rabbi	Chief Rabbi
Archbishop	The Most Reverend and Right Honourable the Lord Archbishop of Fidena	Dear Archbishop	Archbishop	Archbishop of Fidena
The Pope	His Holiness the Pope	Your Holiness	Your Holiness	His Holiness The Pope

The thank-you letter

How to make an abode gemütlich in just three-quarters of an hour; or, 'a daffodil in a milk bottle'

The concept of 'a daffodil in a milk bottle' is that literally any home, temporary or otherwise, can be dramatically improved simply by doing a few small things to make it cosy. This is regardless of whether the dwelling is a post-university starter flat, a family holiday *gîte* in France or a corporate rental in Los Angeles: the principle is the same.

First, tidy up, throw away ruthlessly, and put a daffodil in a (very clean) milk bottle with water in it on the table.

Next, arrange the books on the bookcase so they are not too neat (they need to look used) but are vaguely ordered; buy some mattress-ticking and cut it up to make a table-cloth, a throw or curtains (even if they are nailed up and then tied back with a ribbon); track down a blanket or rug and put it on the chair or sofa; tidy the kitchen, then put out a fresh loaf of bread on a bread board with a bread knife and some fresh coffee in a tin (for the smell alone, even if one does not use it); if possible, have bare boards instead of carpet or lino (if the boards cannot be stripped or polished, they can at least be painted grey or pale blue – although this might be pushing it in three-quarters of an hour, see below); have a pile of newspapers, books, knitting, sewing, anything to make the room look lived in; if there is no furniture, use wooden champagne boxes for anything from a low chair to a side table to a bookshelf; if unable or not allowed to get rid of depressing furniture, cover it with the mattress-ticking; and try to acquire one or two old things – a wooden box, a blue and white plate, a clock, a bentwood chair – as these will improve over time, whereas the cheap, modern stuff will deteriorate into tatt. To this end, it is far better to buy something old at an auction than to buy something new that will look grotty all too soon; magazines like *Country Living* and *BBC Homes & Antiques* are full of ideas.

Above all, aim for simplicity: the chic-est rooms are those that have the confidence not to look as though anyone has tried too hard. And for those who have more than three-quarters of an hour, the next most transforming thing is paint.

Rain
·····································

'1. a. The condensed vapour of the atmosphere, falling in drops large enough to attain a sensible velocity; the fall of such drops.
c. 825 *Vesp. Psalter* cxlvi. 8 Se oferwirð heofen mid wolcnum & gearwað eorðan regn. *a* 1000 ÆLFRIC *Gen.* vii. 4 Ic..sende ren nu..ofer eorðan. 1154 *O.E. Chron.* (Laud MS.) an. 1117 Mid þunre & lihtinge & reine & hagole. *a* 1200 ORMIN 8622 Wel hallf feorþe ȝer..comm na reȝȝn onn eorþe. c 1250 *Gen. & Ex.* 3265 Ðhunder, and leuene, and rein ðor-mong God sent. c 1330 R. BRUNNE *Chron. Wace* (Rolls) 6827 þe arewes come so þykke so reyn. c 1386 CHAUCER *Monk's* T. 183 In reyn with wilde beestes walked hee. ——— *Prioress'* T. 222 Hise salte teeris trickled doun as reyn. c 1449 PECOCK *Repr.* II. Ii. 146 To couere him fro reyne and fro other sturne wedris. 1535 STEWART *Cron. Scot.* III. 257 Fers as ane eill war new tane in the rane. 1635 SWAN *Spec. M.* iv. § 2 (1643) 58 The rain, proceeding from those vapours which we call the clouds. 1710 ADDISON *Tatler* No. 218 ¶ 2 A black Cloud falling to the Earth in long Trails of Rain. 1752 HUME *Ess. & Treat.* (1777) II. 90 There is a certain uniformity in the operation of the sun, rain, and earth. SCOTT *Lady of L.* v. xv, Fierce Roderick..shower'd his blows like wintry rain. 1878 HUXLEY *Physiogr.* 41 We may fairly expect the formation of rain to be preceded by that of cloud.'

Edited from the entry on 'Rain' in the
Oxford English Dictionary

'Goodness, it's rainy today, isn't it?' This is surely the most commonly heard conversation opener in Britain, so one might as well to have something interesting to say in reponse. Although, 'Did you know that the most rainfall ever to fall in a day was on 18 July 1955 in Martinstown in Dorset?' is perhaps not a reply that may ensure the admiring glances of all within earshot, it will at least raise the tone of the conversation up a notch from 'Mmmm, isn't it?'

How rain happens

Water evaporates into the air from oceans, seas, rivers and lakes and also from plants, as well as in small-ish amounts from volcanic gases below ground and from burning fossil fuels above ground. As the water rises upwards, it cools, condensing from a gas to a liquid to form droplets. These droplets then condense around miniscule dust particles; the result is a cloud. Each of the droplets continues to increase in size as new droplets in turn condense onto them. The more this happens, the heavier each droplet becomes, until it is heavy enough to fall from the bottom of the cloud.

However, if the cloud is high, the air dry and warm, or the droplet still small enough that it falls relatively slowly, there is a good chance that it will evaporate entirely before it reaches the ground. Alternatively, it might be caught by an upwards draft of air. In this case, the cycle begins again, the droplets remaining suspended in the atmosphere. The more this happens, the bigger each droplet becomes, which is how really fierce storms are created.

Eventually the droplet becomes so heavy that gravity takes over, regardless of any upwards drafts of air. Even on the way down, it might continue to increase in size as other droplets collide then coalesce with it. The result is that, one way or another, it reaches the ground.

Also note that, technically, rain is only rain when the droplets are more than 0.02 inches (0.5 mm) in diameter. Any smaller and they are classified as drizzle.

In the future, significant changes in UK rainfall patterns are expected, as winters get wetter (and summers get drier). One may as well get used to it – though clearly this is easier said than done when waiting for the bus in one's new suede boots in the midst of a thunderstorm. Be inspired by John Updike's spin on the matter: 'Rain is grace; rain is the sky condescending to the earth; without rain, there would be no life.'

Those who really hate the rain should move to St Osyth in Essex, which is the driest recorded place in the UK with only 513 mm of rainfall a year. Alternatively, splash out on a Marc Jacobs umbrella, which is one of the most fabulous available – they *never* get left on the bus. Trivial as it might appear, an umbrella one adores really can contribute quite considerably to one's everyday level of happiness. For it means that when looking out of the window of a morning, only to see that it is raining *again*, one's reaction shifts from 'Drat, when will it end?' to 'Whoopee, a reason to use my umbrella' – which, on a day-to-day basis, genuinely does make all the difference.

A selection of songs to sing in the rain

'Singing in the Rain' – Gene Kelly
'Raindrops Keep Falling on My Head' – Burt Bacharach
'Rainy Days and Mondays' – The Carpenters
'Purple Rain' – Prince
'Why Does it Always Rain On Me?' – Travis
'Don't Rain on My Parade' – Barbra Streisand
'November Rain' – Guns 'n' Roses
'It's Raining Men'– The Weather Girls
'Raining in My Heart' – Buddy Holly
'Here Comes The Rain Again' – The Eurythmics
'A Hard Rain's Gonna Fall' – Bob Dylan[1]
'Another Fucking Song About the Rain' – Daniel Johnston & Jack Medicine

1 Some might prefer the Roxy Music version.

Diets

....

The country's first truly popular fad diet was invented by William Banting, a rotund nineteenth-century casket-maker who, at an advanced stage in life, was appalled to discover that he was no longer able to reach down to tie his own shoe-laces, such was his girth. His doctor advised him to give up his usual intake of bread, butter, milk, sugar, beer and potatoes, owing to the fact it contained too much 'starch and saccharine matter, tending to create fat, and should be avoided altogether'. Banting followed this advice and made some radical changes to his eating regime, changes later detailed in his *Letter on Corpulence*. Published in 1863, it was Britain's first best-selling, low-carb diet, selling over 63,000 copies by the time of the fourth edition.

An extract from a 'Letter on Corpulence' by William Banting (1863)

For breakfast, at 9 a.m., I take five to six ounces of either beef mutton, kidneys, broiled fish, bacon, or cold meat of any kind except pork or veal; a large cup of tea or coffee (without milk or sugar), a little biscuit, or one ounce of dry toast; making together six ounces solid, nine liquid.

For dinner, at 2 p.m. Five or six ounces of any fish except salmon, herrings, or eels, any meat except pork or veal, any vegetable except potato, parsnip, beetroot, turnip, or carrot, one ounce of dry toast, fruit out of a pudding not sweetened, any kind of poultry or game, and two or three glasses of good claret, sherry, or Madeira – Champagne, port, and beer forbidden; making together ten to twelve ounces solid, and ten liquid.

For tea, at 6 p.m. Two or three ounces of cooked fruit, a rusk or two, and a cup of tea without milk or sugar; making two to four ounces solid, nine liquid.

For supper, at 9 p.m. Three or four ounces of meat or fish, similar to dinner, with a glass or two of claret or sherry and water; making four ounces solid and seven liquid.

For nightcap, if required. A tumbler of grog – (gin, whisky, or brandy, without sugar) – or a glass or two of claret or sherry.

The world's worst diets

Atkins diet

Inventor	Date invented	Textbook
Robert C. Atkins	1972	*Dr Atkins' Diet Revolution* (1972); *Dr Atkins' New Diet Revolution* (1992)

The ultimate modern low-carb, high-protein diet. Any diet that drives its devotees to carry slices of ham and cheese around in their jacket pockets, while at the same time forbidding them to eat carrots or beetroot, is clearly a preposterous one.

Despite this, even perfectly intelligent people have been known to give it a go. This is because it does work – but only in the short-term, and with side effects including body odour and heart problems.

Slimfast

Inventor	Date invented	Textbook
S. Daniel Abraham	1977	slimfast.co.uk

A Slimfast milkshake for breakfast and lunch, followed by a 'normal' supper. Fine for those happy to subsist primarily on milkshakes, but otherwise . . .

Grapefruit Diet

Inventor	Date invented
No single person or organisation has claimed credit, though it was certainly popularised by a number of now-forgotten Hollywood starlets	1930s

Eat half a grapefruit with every meal. Much more effective is half a pineapple, however. See below.

Beverly Hills Diet

Inventor	Date invented	Textbook
Judy Mazel	1981	*The Beverly Hills Diet* (1981), followed by *The New Beverly Hills Diet* (1996), both by Judy Mazel

In which pineapple is to be eaten with every meal (interchanged occasionally with mango and papaya). This does actually work. Pineapple is the only creation of Nature's to contain an enzyme called bromelein, which basically digests protein – in other words, it eats away at fat. It is not a particularly healthy way to lose weight, however.

Cabbage Soup Diet

Inventor	Date invented
Again, no single person or organisation has claimed credit.	Mid-1990s

Eat as much cabbage soup as you like per day! Only for dimwits. Or for those who enjoy breaking wind.

The world's best diet

There is only one diet that actually works in the long term. It is this: eat less unhealthy food, eat more healthy food, take more exercise. It is not rocket science. When one wants to over-indulge, fine, great, but over-indulge on delicious ratatouille with brown rice, on juicy strawberries or on sweet edamame. And do not do it every day. And do some exercise in between. Dull it may be, but it also, annoyingly, works.

The muses

In Greek mythology, the muses are the nine goddess daughters of Zeus, king of the gods, and Mnemosyne, the goddess of memory. They preside over the arts and sciences, ready and able at any moment to inspire artists, poets, philosophers and musicians all around the world to produce great works. Some might call this a dull job; but to others, it represents the pinnacle of a lifetime's aspiration.

Name	Muse of . . .	Emblem*
Calliope	Epic song	A writing tablet.
Clio	History	A scroll and books
Erato	Love or erotic poetry	A lyre and a crown
Euterpe	Lyric song	A flute
Melpomene	Tragedy	A tragic mask
Polyhymnia	Sacred song. Sometimes also geometry, mime, meditation and agriculture.	A pensive expression
Terpsichore	Dance	Dancing and carrying a lyre
Thalia	Comedy	A comic mask
Urania	Astronomy	A staff and a celestial globe

* A prop or pose used to distinguish one muse from another when depicting them in art, particularly Roman, Renaissance and Neoclassical art.

How to use a compass

Travellers were once limited to using the position of the celestial bodies to guide them. Since then methods have evolved to become rather less romantic, if more accurate. About a thousand years ago, the earliest recorded accounts of the use of a compass appeared in China, where it took the form of a magnetic needle floating in a bowl of water. In the modern age, we are blessed with A–Zs, websites such as Streetmap or Mapquest, and global positioning systems. Nonetheless, an ability to use a compass remains a key survival skill for anyone considering setting forth into the jungle – concrete or otherwise.

compass needle   orienting lines   compass housing   direction-of-travel arrow

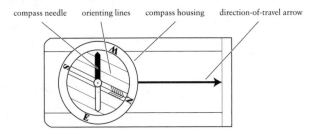

The most important thing to remember is that the red arrow inside a compass always points to magnetic North. Confusion can often arise from the idea that it will somehow be adjusted to point in the direction one wishes to go. But it does not, it *only ever* points North, and one establishes one's route in relation to this.

If North is not the desired bearing, there are two ways of using a compass, either with a map, which will give a more accurate direction, or without a map, which is the most basic method, and the one covered here.

Around the edge of the compass is a moveable ring marked with N, S, E and W for North, South, East and West. This is called the 'compass housing'. So to go south-east, for example, rotate the ring until the halfway point between S and E is aligned with the 'direction of travel' arrow.

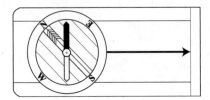

Hold the compass flat, then turn one's body until the red compass needle is aligned with the parallel lines inside the compass housing. It is *extremely* important that the red end of the needle is pointing at the end marked 'N' (rather than 'S') – otherwise one will set off 180 degrees in the wrong direction. Now walk in the direction of the 'direction of travel' arrow, keeping the needle at all times within the parallel lines, and one will be walking south-east.

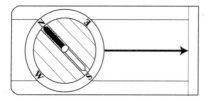

Then let the adventure begin.

(See page 87 for the correct footwear for the adventure in question.)

Ten good ideas

Idea	Year	Inventor	Nationality
Flush toilet	1589	Sir John Harington	England
Braille	1829	Louis Braille	France
Safety pin	1849	Walter Hunt	U.S.A.
Paper clip	1900	Johann Waaler	Norway
Frozen food	1923	Clarence Birdseye	U.S.A.
Launderette	1934	J.F.Cantrell	U.S.A.
Mobile phone	1947	Richard Frenkiel & Joel Engel of Bell Labs	U.S.A.[1]
Contact lenses	1948	Kevin Tuohy	U.S.A.
The Pill	1954	Gregory Pincus & John Rock	U.S.A.
Post-it note	1980	Art Fry of 3M	U.S.A.

1 It is open to debate whether the mobile phone fits into this category; many might argue otherwise.

A few Second World War heroines

....

Ala Gertner (?1912–1945)

Ala Gertner was born in Bedzin in southern Poland into a wealthy Jewish family. In 1940, she was instructed to report to a nearby train station. She was transported to Geppersdorf, a Nazi labour camp, where she worked in the administrative office. A year later she was allowed home for a visit, but swiftly secured a posting at the local Judenrat (the Jewish civilian government), thus extending her leave indefinitely. Happily, marriage to Bernard Holtz – who had worked at the desk next to hers in Geppersdorf – followed soon after.

About a month later, Ala became one of the last group of Jews in the area to be deported – this time, to Auschwitz. At the camp, she worked in the warehouse, sorting the possessions of Jews who had been gassed; before long she was reassigned to the munitions factory. It was here that she became involved in a conspiracy to steal gunpowder out of the factory and smuggle it to the prisoners, whose job it was to burn and bury corpses from the gas chambers. Their intention was to blow up one of the crematoriums, in turn sparking off a camp uprising.

On 7 October 1944, one of the crematoriums was successfully detonated and several SS guards were shot. It was the only armed uprising ever to occur at Auschwitz.

It did not last long. Some of the men involved managed to escape after the uprising, but they were soon caught and shot. Ala and the other three women involved – Ester Wajcblum, Regina Safirsztayn and Roza Robota – were accused of sabotage, resistance and treason. On 5 January 1945 they were all hanged – just twenty-two days before the camp was liberated by the Red Army.

Sophie Scholl (1921–1943)

Sophie Scholl was the fourth of five children born into a middle-class, liberal, deeply Christian family, in 1942 Sophie Scholl embarked upon a degree in philosophy and biology at Munich University. Her brother, Hans, was a student there at the same time, and it was through him that she met many of her friends. That summer, she was obliged to enrol for war work at a metallurgical plant; around the same time, her father was sent to jail for making critical remarks about Hitler. These events galvanised her into joining the White Rose, a movement recently formed by Hans that advocated passive resistance to the Nazis: 'We want to try to show that everyone is in a position to contribute to the overthrow of the system . . . it can be done only by the cooperation of many convinced, energetic people . . .' The White Rose's foremost tactic was to produce leaflets that attacked the Nazis and called for the restoration of a democratic government. These were distributed throughout central Germany, in particular to bar owners and university lecturers, both of whom were thought to be central to spreading the word.

On 18 February 1943 Sophie and Hans were distributing leaflets throughout their university building when they suddenly realised they were about to run out of time before classes finished for the day. Sophie raced upstairs to a third-floor landing and flung all of the remaining leaflets through the air into an inner courtyard below – she later put the decision down to 'either high spirits or stupidity'. As students filed out of the lecture halls, the leaflets lay scattered all over the floor. Sophie and Hans were spotted by a local handyman who was also a member of the Nazi party, and who called the police.

Sophie explained her involvement in the White Rose: 'Somebody, after all, had to make a start. What we wrote and said is also believed by many others. They just do not dare express themselves as we did.' Just four days after their arrest, Sophie, Hans and their friend Christoph Probst were condemned to death for treason. At five o'clock the same day, they were guillotined.

Odette Brailly/Sansom/Hallowes/Churchill (1912–1995)

Odette Brailly was born in France and moved to Britain in 1931 when she married an Englishman. When war broke out, she felt compelled to find a way to help: 'My father was killed thirty days before the Armistice in World War One. My mother was still in France in 1939. I had the idea that I must do anything to help to save France from the Germans.' This was despite the fact that she had three young daughters still at school. She volunteered at the War Office, which at the time was desperate to recruit anyone fluent in French. She ended up a member of the Special Operations Executive (SOE), alongside other exceptionally brave, soon-to-be undercover agents like Violette Szabo, Nancy Wake and Noor Inayat Kahn.

In 1942, after undergoing intensive training, Odette was posted to France to act as a liaison between the Resistance movement and SOE agents. She posed as 'Lise', a French widow, and based herself in Marseilles where she couriered messages between agents. She was also responsible for finding safe houses to enable her commanding officer, Peter Churchill, to send radio messages.

But in April 1943, Odette was betrayed. She and Churchill were arrested by the Gestapo, interrogated at length, and tortured – it was thought, correctly, that she knew much more than she was letting on about the workings of the radio operators. Odette gave nothing away, thus saving many, many lives, as well as allowing the Resistance movement to continue its heroic struggle.

Odette was eventually sent to Ravensbrück concentration camp, where she was thrown into a cell adjacent to the torture chamber. The

A few Second World War heroines

noises she heard there haunted her for life. The only reason she was not executed was that she and Churchill had managed to convince their captors not only that they were married, but also that he was related to Winston Churchill.

A few months after D-Day, as Soviet troops advanced towards Ravensbruck, Odette escaped from the camp by hijacking a car, and persuading the driver, who happened to be the camp commander, to take her to the nearby American base. He had hoped that she in turn might help save him from the Soviets. But she did not, and the Americans arrested him, put him on trial, and hanged him.

After the war, Odette was awarded an MBE and the George Cross. Odette later said of her fellow SOE operatives: 'They are all our mothers and sisters, you would not be able to either learn or play in freedom today, yes, you may not even have been born, if such women had not stood their soft, slender bodies before you and your future like protective steel shields throughout the Fascist terrors.' She died in Walton-on-Thames in 1995 at the age of eighty-two.

Victoria Scherautz (1916–2006)[1]

Born into an aristocratic Warsaw family, Victoria initially studied to be a painter. In 1938 she married a young politician, Alexander Scherautz, but when war broke out just a year later, they were both arrested. After three weeks aboard a cattle train, Victoria found herself under orders to start work on the construction of the Trans-Siberian railway – laying piece of track after piece of track in freezing temperatures in the depths of the Siberian forest. Before long, she had the idea of using bricks made out of frozen mud to build makeshift huts. What resulted was a little village of huts to shelter in through the harsh winter. The response of the Soviet authorities, predictably enough, was to torture her, one result of which was that she was never able to have children.

In 1941 the Soviet Union was invaded by the Nazis, and Victoria was released, along with many of her fellow Polish prisoners. As the cattle train chugged out of the train station, scores of babies were thrown on board by women who were too weak to travel themselves, but who desperately wanted to give their children a chance of survival. Victoria caught one such baby just as his mother shouted over the noise of the engine, 'His name is Yurek!'

Victoria and Yurek then escaped overland in the company of General Anders' expedition of 70,000 Polish soldiers and civilians who were marching overland into the Middle East, eventually to join the allied forces in Italy. Stopping off in India, Victoria established an orphanage for exiled Polish children. Her long-term aim, however, was to join the Polish army in Iran, where she hoped she might track down

1 Victoria's story only finally came to light with the publication in the *Guardian* (21 June 2006) of an obituary written by her nephew.

her husband, also an ex-POW. Embarking on this journey meant that she was forced to put Yurek up for adoption, and he was given to a wealthy Indian couple.

Victoria eventually made it to Iran, where she and Alexander were reunited. From then on, she worked variously for the Polish diplomatic missions and in organising supplies for the British army in north Africa, until the war ended and the couple moved to London.

While she was en route to attend General Anders' funeral in 1970, something extraordinary happened. On the plane, Victoria overheard a man in the seat behind her vividly describing to another passenger how, as a baby, a woman called Victoria had rescued him from a work camp in Siberia. From then on he had always considered her to be his mother; he even vaguely remembered her giving him up for adoption, an inevitably traumatic experience. He had ended up in England, graduated from Edinburgh University and had become a doctor. All that time he had continued to hope he might one day be reunited with his mother. He still did.

Victoria, however, decided not to make herself known to Yurek. He was in his early thirties; he was accompanied by his pregnant wife; he had his whole life ahead of him, which she did not want to disrupt. She was simply relieved to know that he was alive and prospering. According to her nephew Wiktor Grodecki she always said it was the happiest moment of her life

Vere Hodgson (1901–1979)

Vere Hodgson may not have been an SOE operative or a resistance fighter, but she represents all those women who were left behind on the home front during the war and who attempted to continue to live 'normal' lives. Just as brave in their own way as many of those who were on the front line, there was no way that the likes of Vere were going to let Hitler disrupt all that they knew and loved about the British way of life. Day-to-day, Vere helped run a charity in Notting Hill Gate, but from June 1940 onwards she also kept a diary which was later published under the title *Few Eggs and No Oranges*, a vivid account of what it was like for women like her to live through the Blitz. The early pages in particular demonstrate that even in the midst of unimaginable awfulness, life goes on – it has to:

7 November 1940

A terrible night! Guns never seemed to cease. Many bombs. No chance to go up the road. Slept at office until All Clear after 7 a.m. Not very refreshing to sleep in one's clothes, but the lovely bath helps a bit. Every district of London got it last night . . . .Very difficult to get any eggs . . . almost impossible. Not a kipper to be had for a long time. Can't think what they have done with them . . . With regard to news on the Home Front, as if there was not enough to do, the Cat was taken ill! He was ailing before Xmas – could not jump on a chair. I fetched the vet. Between us we poured some liquid paraffin down his throat . . . I put the little animal up on a shelf near some warm pipes. He seems better.

31 January 1941

Yesterday there was much going on above us and gunfire. Mrs Starmer came back full of news of incendiaries in the City at Moorgate. The people rose out of the ground in droves to put them out! Everybody was laughing at the fun. She said it was like a football match and all enjoyed themselves.

A lady in the Mercury Café told me she was having lunch in Oxford Street Suddenly a terrific wonk shook the place; all the cups and saucers danced and rattled about on the table. The man opposite her said calmly: 'That was a bomb, wasn't it?' She replied: 'I'm sure it was.' And they continued to eat their meal.

How humans spread

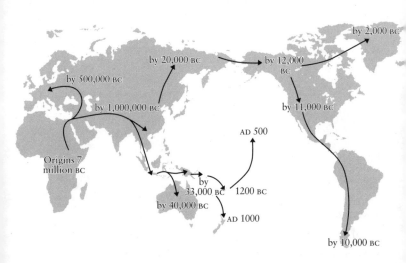

Inspired by figure 1.1 in Guns, Germs and Steel *by Jared Diamond (1977).*

Long-term investing

There is no doubt that the concept of investing is, to most of us, too dull even to contemplate before the age of about a hundred and six. But if one takes a moment to make a few calculations about how much money could actually be accumulated without too much trouble, it suddenly becomes a whole lot more interesting – a whole lot more, in fact, like a route to buying that château in the South of France one's always dreamed about. The table below reveals the amount of money accumulated over fifty years if one were to invest £52 a year (i.e. £1 per week) into various kinds of investment programmes. It makes one's daily cappuccino (cost: £1.75, and that's without a smile) suddenly begin to seem like sheer madness . . .

	A savings account at a bank or building society[1]	Stocks & shares[2]	Government bonds (also known as 'gilts')[3]	Property[4]	Art[5]	Betting on horses[6]	Under the bed
1 year on	52	52	52	52	52	52	52
2 years on	104	107	105	105	105	101	104
3 years on	158	165	159	159	159	147	156
4 years on	212	227	214	214	215	191	208
5 years on	267	293	270	270	272	232	260
10 years on	554	685	569	569	579	408	520
25 years on	1,543	2,852	1,665	1,665	1753	715	1,300
50 years on	3,729	15,097	4,398	4,398	4,925	889	2,600

Note that the big difference in returns really happens between twenty-five and fifty years. The upshot is that skimping on cappuccinos can help one build up a significant nest-egg over a long period of time. So if the plan is to move to a château on retirement, marvellous. However, for those who plan to move to the house in France significantly in advance of retirement (i.e. within the next ten years or so), there are various alternative options:

• Very serious saving, at the expense not just of cappuccinos but all sorts of other pleasures

• Earning pots of money

• Becoming a very skilled or very lucky short-term investor

But beware – history is not, the actuaries now believe, a good guide to the future. The rates quoted above may be an overestimate of what one can now expect. Yields have been coming down (a result of the success of the world economy), creating a crisis for pension funds. In other words, it is a very inexact science unless one is able to see into the future; hence it is also worth considering completely ignoring all the above suggestions, and going to see an independent financial adviser instead.

1 Assuming that the average real return per annum is 1.4% (source: Barclays Equity Gilt Study). There are various points, however, to bear in mind: the long-term average always includes all sorts of cycles; the effects of inflation have to be factored in (i.e. with inflation at 2.4% at the end of 2006, those whose interest rate is claimed by the bank to be, say, 4.5% are actually receiving a real interest return of 2.1% – in other words, not as great as it sounds); and do not forget that bank interest is taxed, so the real return becomes lower still. All in all, it is a tricky business, and it is these very complexities that keep financial advisers rich and able to pay their children's school fees.

2 Assuming that the average real return per annum is 6% (source: appendix C of the 2005 report of the UK Pensions Commission). Again, there are various points to bear in mind: the transaction costs for stocks and shares tend to be high; the return on stocks and shares is made up of the increase in capital value *plus* the dividends; and, finally, most in the financial world are predicting that the real return per annum is likely to fall very soon to more like 4.5%.

3 Assuming that the average real return per annum is 2% (source: appendix C of the 2005 report of the UK Pensions Commission). As with stocks and shares, the transaction costs for government bonds tend to be high.

4 Assuming that (in the long-term, as ever) the average real return per annum on UK residential property is 2% (source: appendix C of the 2005 report of the UK Pensions Commission). Do not be seduced by dinner-party chat. Houses, as investments, are not as good as equity. However, since the equity return is made up of the increase in capital value plus the dividends, if one regards living in a house as a dividend then the long-term returns may be roughly the same – that is, quite good. What is quite surprising is that UK real house-price increases average roughly the same as government bonds. Of course, this is an average – it will be less in Scotland and more in London – but, in practice, many are carried away by recent fast rises in London, which are due to special conditions.

5 Assuming that the average real return per annum is 2.4% (source: 'Accounting for Taste: Art and the Financial Markets over Three Centuries' by W.N. Goetzman in *American Economic Review* Volume 83), but this is contested. Some research suggests that the return is slightly better than equities, and that it has the additional advantage of diversification; others suggest that sale prices are not a true index because they conceal not only high transaction costs, but also all the art which never gets sold (and instead just sits in the attic).

6 Assuming that the average real return per annum is −5.5% (source: Gavyn Davies in the *Guardian*, 27 July 2006, drawing on analysis of 6,301,016 horse-races between 1992 and 2001). Bear in mind, however, that this only applies if one bets just on the favourites; if one bets on the medium favourites (3/1 to 15/1), the return will be closer to −18%.

How to deliver a baby

Don't panic must be the watchword; and don't try to be a midwife either, if you can avoid it. The following suggestions are for those who have either tried to get the mother to hospital or have called for medical help but the baby has beaten everyone to it. If so, proceed as follows:

Lay the mother on the ground on top of whatever the cleanest thing to hand is – sheets ideally. Being on the ground also ensures that when the baby arrives, he or she does not slide or slip off anywhere. Put a pillow, makeshift or otherwise, under the mother's hips, as well as one under her back. Wash your hands as thoroughly as possible, after which you should avoid touching anything except for the mother, the baby and the sheets. This is to prevent infection.

Next, peer between the mother's legs. As soon as the baby's head becomes visible, birth is imminent. There is a chance that the head will still be covered by the amniotic sac, a membrane-like substance – in which case, burst the membrane by pinching then twisting it out of the way, thus releasing the amniotic fluid.

Everything will then start to speed up. Put your hand under the baby's head to guide it, making sure it does not shoot out too fast, but equally that it keeps on coming. As it comes out, it should naturally turn on to the side. If this is all happening, let nature take its course as much as possible.

Once the baby's head is out, wipe away fluid from the baby's mouth and nose to help it breathe. If the umbilical cord is wrapped around the baby's neck, try to slip it over the baby's head.

Guide, but do not pull, the shoulders out. The baby will then slide right out. Check the breathing, then wrap him or her up warmly, leaving the face uncovered.

Do not forget about the placenta, which appears afterwards, and which also needs to be delivered.

Sailing

Have no illusions: sailing is not for the delicate of disposition. So before accepting an invitation to spend the day at sea, be sure to find out exactly what sort of trip is planned. Will you be required merely to lounge around in a bikini drinking cocktails, the most pressing matter of the day being which factor sun-cream to use? Or, conversely, will you be expected to act as a member of the crew?

If the latter, the principal challenge will be to attempt to follow a succession of all-but-incomprehensible instructions, usually shouted at you through the wind and rain as you slide from one side of the boat to the other, not unlike a flailing puppy. For to bestow upon someone the title of 'ship's captain' for the day is to have them morph before your eyes from a calm and rational member of the human race into a ranting lunatic. Tales abound within the sailing community of crew members seen suddenly jumping overboard and swimming to shore with just a single backward glance to yell 'I want a divorce' at the ship's captain (aka the husband), after being shouted at one too many times for having yanked at the main sheet rather than the spinnaker – or whatever. So be warned.

Some other sailing tips include: pee before embarking. Be sure to take extra hair pins, as well as sunglasses, for within an hour they will have fallen off and become bent or broken. Hold on tightly. And be patient, even when the trip turns out to last a little longer than expected: Ellen McArthur was at sea for over seventy-one days in order to break the record for the fastest solo non-stop circumnavigation of the world, and even she admits to crying a couple of times.

The terminology

fore: front.

aft: back.

bow: the front of the hull.

stern: the back of the hull.

boom: a horizontal pole used to support rigging that threatens to knock a beginner unconscious at any opportunity. Beware.

port: the left-hand side of the boat when facing forward.

starboard: the right-hand side of the boat when facing forward.

port tack: the wind is on the port side.

starboard tack: the wind is on the starboard side.

to tack: to turn the bow of the boat through the wind so that the boat changes direction.

to jibe (or gybe): to turn the stern of the boat through the wind so that the boat changes direction.

windward: towards the wind.

leeward: away from the wind.

stand-on: one's own boat has the right of way, so maintain speed and course.

give way: the approaching boat has right of way, so alter speed and course to avoid it.

bulkhead / ceiling: wall.

overheads: ceiling.

deck / sole: floor.

head: loo.

galley: kitchen.

line: rope. This is one aspect of sailing that an ignorance of which seems particularly to irritate experienced sailors. It may seem dull, but it is really important. A line means a rope, and onboard each line has a particular purpose. Any that are attached to sails to control their shapes are known as sheets; so, for instance, the main sheet is the line that controls the main sail and the spinnaker sheet is the line that controls the spinnaker (the large triangular sail at the front of the boat). A line that raises a sail is a halyard, but one that lowers it is a downhaul or a Cunningham. A line used to tie up the boat is a dockline.

Frequently heard instructions

These tend to concern modifying the direction of the boat in order to respond to the direction of the wind. If the captain (or whoever is at the helm) shouts 'Ready to tack?', the correct response is to shout back just as gustily, 'Ready!' Similarly, 'Ready to jibe?' demands a 'Ready!' Also crucial to comprehend is 'make fast that line!', which translates as 'tie up that rope!' – an instruction that is particularly welcome when heard near the dock because it usually means that the trip is at an end and a gin and tonic at the sailing club bar is at last within reach.

The window box

....

Nothing transforms the look of a house or a flat as much as a colourful, blooming window box. Conversely, there is nothing as depressing as the sight of a dead window box. It costs so little, takes so little time and so little effort, yet can have such a great effect – it is really, really worth doing.

The window box itself should be wooden, lead or plain earthenware (never plastic). Twice a year, take a trip to a garden centre to buy plants and (although you only need to do this once a year) some soil to add to the existing soil – the older, grottier-looking stuff needs to be spooned out and replaced with fresh. In September, plant the first bulbs: daffodils are the easiest, while tulips are also worth considering (although see below about going native) as long as there are no squirrels around, in which case forget it. Plant the daffodil bulbs about two or three inches down; above them and spaced three inches apart in between them, try winter-flowering pansies (all in one colour if you want to be truly chic). The difficult bit is getting the plants out of the polystyrene containers – a knife helps. The pansies will last for a couple of months, during which time they need to be watered once a week if it does not rain; those who can be bothered may also want to add a teaspoon of liquid fertiliser to the water.

When the pansies have had it, throw them away and replace them with some common box plants (this is a type of plant, by the way, not advice on where to grow it, as the more amateur gardeners amongst us might suppose – its proper name is *Buxus sempervirens*), either on their own or interspersed with red bobbly plants known as winter cherries or *Capiscum solanum*.

In the spring, the daffodils will start to come up. When they do, dig up the spent *solanum* and throw them away; it is also worth considering digging up the box plants and moving them elsewhere, it being a bit dull to have evergreens like these all year round. A fallow period then follows for a while, during which some coloured primulas (planted when flowering) are just the thing: they do not last long but are very jolly while they do. These may be planted on top of the daffodil bulbs, which at this stage will also need a bit of attention in the form of some liquid fertiliser if the bulbs are to have any chance of flowering the following year.

May is then the month to plant petunias or geraniums. Again, these should all be in the same colour. Once a week, one has to pinch off the dead flowers so that new ones grow; but this is actually rather fun and therapeutic and only takes a couple of minutes. They then last until September, when everything but the daffodils should be dug up. The whole cycle then begins again.

A few general points to note are: generally, it does not matter overly much whether the window box is placed in the sun or the shade; everything should be planted fairly close together – two or three inches apart, perhaps; and water once a week unless it rains, in which case, don't bother.

Finally, in an ideal world, one would ensure that all the plants chosen for the window box are native (tulips, for instance, are not, they are from Turkey). One of the main reasons for this is that native plants tend to require the least maintenance, adapted as they are already to local soils and climate. In addition, it is important that everyone does their bit to conserve Britain's flora in the face of so much destruction elsewhere of the natural environment. To find out which plants are native to your area, consult the database at the website of the Natural History Museum (nhm.ac.uk/fff).

British native plants beginning with the letter 'a'

Latin name	Common name
Acer campestre	Field Maple
Aceras anthropophorum	Man Orchid
Achillea millefolium	Yarrow
Achillea ptarmica	Sneezewort
Aconitum napellus	Monk's-hood
Actaea spicata	Baneberry
Adiantum capillus-veneris	Maidenhair Fern
Adoxa moschatellina	Moschatel

Latin name	Common name
Aethusa cynapium	Fool's Parsley
Agrimonia eupatoria	Agrimony
Agrimonia procera	Fragrant Agrimony
Agrostis canina	Velvet Bent
Agrostis capillaris	Common Bent
Agrostis curtisii	Bristle Bent
Agrostis gigantea	Black Bent
Agrostis stolonifera	Creeping Bent
Agrostis vinealis	Brown Bent
Aira caryophyllea	Silver Hair-grass
Aira praecox	Early Hair-grass
Ajuga chamaepitys	Ground-pine
Ajuga pyramidalis	Pyramidal Bugle
Ajuga reptans	Bugle
Alchemilla alpina	Alpine Lady's-mantle
Alchemilla filicaulis	Hairy Lady's-mantle
Alchemilla glabra	Smooth Lady's-mantle
Alchemilla xanthochlora	Intermediate Lady's-mantle
Alisma gramineum	Ribbon-leaved Water-plantain
Alisma lanceolatum	Narrow-leaved Water-plantain
Alisma plantago-aquatica	Water-plantain
Alliaria petiolata	Garlic Mustard
Allium ampeloprasum	Wild Leek
Allium oleraceum	Field Garlic
Allium schoenoprasum	Chives
Allium scorodoprasum	Sand Leek
Allium sphaerocephalon	Round-headed Leek
Allium ursinum	Ramsons
Allium vineale	Wild Onion
Alnus glutinosa	Alder
Alopecurus aequalis	Orange Foxtail
Alopecurus borealis	Alpine Foxtail
Alopecurus bulbosus	Bulbous Foxtail
Alopecurus geniculatus	Marsh Foxtail
Alopecurus myosuroides	Black-grass
Alopecurus pratensis	Meadow Foxtail
Althaea officinalis	Marsh-mallow
Ammophila arenaria	Marram
Anacamptis pyramidalis	Pyramidal Orchid

Latin name	Common name
Anagallis arvensis	Scarlet Pimpernel
Anagallis minima	Chaffweed
Anagallis tenella	Bog Pimpernel
Anchusa arvensis	Bugloss
Andromeda polifolia	Bog-rosemary
Anemone nemorosa	Wood Anemone
Angelica sylvestris	Wild Angelica
Anisantha sterilis	Barren Brome
Anogramma leptophylla	Jersey Fern
Antennaria dioica	Mountain Everlasting
Anthemis arvensis	Corn Chamomile
Anthemis cotula	Stinking Chamomile
Anthoxanthum odoratum	Sweet Vernal-grass
Anthriscus caucalis	Bur Chervil
Anthriscus sylvestris	Cow Parsley
Anthyllis vulneraria	Kidney Vetch
Apera interrupta	Dense Silky-bent
Apera spica-venti	Loose Silky-bent
Aphanes arvensis	Parsley-piert
Aphanes inexspectata	Slender Parsley-piert
Apium graveolens	Wild Celery
Apium inundatum	Lesser Marshwort
Apium nodiflorum	Fool's water-cress
Apium repens	Creeping Marshwort
Aquilegia vulgaris	Columbine
Arabidopsis thaliana	Thale Cress
Arabis alpina	Alpine Rock-cress
Arabis glabra	Tower Mustard
Arabis hirsuta	Hairy Rock-cress
Arabis petraea	Northern Rock-cress
Arabis scabra	Bristol Rock-cress
Arbutus unedo	Strawberry-tree
Arctium lappa	Greater Burdock
Arctium minus	Lesser Burdock
Arctostaphylos alpinus	Alpine Bearberry
Arctostaphylos uva-ursi	Bearberry
Arenaria ciliata	Fringed Sandwort
Arenaria norvegica	Arctic Sandwort
Arenaria serpyllifolia	Thyme-leaved Sandwort
Armeria arenaria	Jersey Thrift

Latin name	Common name
Armeria maritima	Thrift
Arnoseris minima	Lamb's Succory
Arrhenatherum elatius	False Oat-grass
Artemisia absinthium	Wormwood
Artemisia campestris	Field Wormwood
Artemisia norvegica	Norwegian Mugwort
Artemisia vulgaris	Mugwort
Arum italicum	Italian Lords-and-Ladies
Arum maculatum	Lords-and-Ladies
Asparagus officinalis	Wild Asparagus
Asperula cynanchica	Squinancywort
Asplenium adiantum-nigrum	Black Spleenwort
Asplenium marinum	Sea Spleenwort
Asplenium obovatum	Lanceolate Spleenwort
Asplenium onopteris	Irish Spleenwort
Asplenium ruta-muraria	Wall-rue
Asplenium septentrionale	Forked Spleenwort
Asplenium trichomanes	Maidenhair Spleenwort
Asplenium trichomanes-ramosum	Green Spleenwort
Aster linosyris	Goldilocks Aster
Aster tripolium	Sea Aster
Astragalus alpinus	Alpine Milk-vetch
Astragalus danicus	Purple Milk-vetch
Astragalus glycyphyllos	Wild Liquorice
Athyrium distentifolium	Alpine Lady-fern
Athyrium filix-femina	Lady-fern
Athyrium flexile	Newman's Lady-fern
Atriplex glabriuscula	Babington's Orache
Atriplex laciniata	Frosted Orache
Atriplex littoralis	Grass-leaved Orache
Atriplex longipes	Long-stalked Orache
Atriplex patula	Common Orache
Atriplex pedunculata	Pedunculate Sea-purslane
Atriplex portulacoides	Sea-purslane
Atriplex praecox	Early Orache
Atriplex prostrata	Spear-leaved Orache
Atropa belladonna	Deadly Nightshade

Source: Natural History Museum.

Towards Helen of Troy

....

UK spending on beauty products in 2005 in £s

Perfume	96,638,000
Toilet water	126,698,000
Lip make-up	68,751,000
Eye make-up	80,930,000
Manicure or pedicure preparations	38,923,000
Powders (including talcum powder)	31,997,000
All other beauty, make-up and skin care preparations other than the above (including body lotions, cleansers and sun cream)	377,748,000
Shampoos	282,011,000
Preparations for permanent straightening or waving of hair	537,000
Hair lacquers	23,214,000
All other hair preparations	97,059,000
Dentifrice (including toothpaste and denture cleaners)	88,964,000
All other oral hygiene preparations (including mouthwash and denture fixative pastes)	47,631,000
Pre-shave, shaving and after-shave preparations	48,277,000
Deodorants and anti-perspirants	211,180,000
Bath preparations	204,158,000
All other beauty products (including depilatories and contact lens solutions)	13,179,000
Total	**1,837,895,000**

Source: Office of National Statistics

£1,837,895,000? It's an awful lot of money, isn't it? One alternative is simply to throw out all the extraneous beauty products that were purchased many moons ago in the hope they would magically: a) make you look like Audrey Hepburn, b) get you a promotion, and c) get you more sex, but that now tend to mope at the back of the bathroom cupboard, and gallivant off to a salon for the afternoon instead. Some of the treatments offered at a salon are similarly based on piffle, but at least it is the kind of piffle that allows you to relax for an hour or two without the telephone tinkling or the children screeching. Ninety-two million visits are made to salons every year, which averages out at just under three per woman (not counting the men who increasingly frequent such places), so somebody somewhere thinks it is a good idea, clearly.

The beauty salon

Some women are devoted to the salon; to others, however, it represents a nightmarish world of embarrassment and confusion. For those who fall into the latter category, there is one particular conundrum that dominates: Pants, Or No Pants? 'Tis indeed a tricky one. A good beauty therapist will give clear instructions unprompted, but there are times when such instructions fail to materialise (often when one is abroad), at which point a fall-back position is required, which is: if in doubt, keep the Pants on. This applies generally, in fact.

However, to feel healthier, happier, more relaxed and more glowing inside and out than all the above put together can make one, try a course of acupuncture. It takes a little perseverance – about four to six sessions are generally required before discernible improvements are felt. But these tend to be dramatic. Recent research has shown acupuncture's efficacy in treating back pain, migraines, morning sickness, arthritis, digestive problems, allergies, insomnia, and, in particular, problems conceiving. A branch known as 'five element acupuncture' is particularly great for an all-round physical and emotional MOT that addresses low spirits generally. That our Western brains sometimes find it a little difficult to compute how this ancient Chinese technique actually works is not what is important here. The fact is that it does. For a list of reputable practitioners, contact the British Acupuncture Council at acupuncture.org.uk or 0208 735 0400.

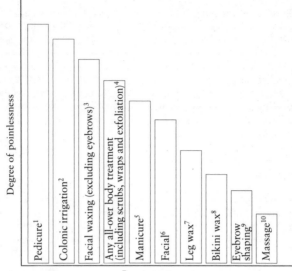

Degree of pointlessness

Beauty treatment

Pedicure[1]

Colonic irrigation[2]

Facial waxing (excluding eyebrows)[3]

Any all-over body treatment (including scrubs, wraps and exfoliation)[4]

Manicure[5]

Facial[6]

Leg wax[7]

Bikini wax[8]

Eyebrow shaping[9]

Massage[10]

1 No. A pedicure is a waste of a life. Life is too short to worry about the way one's feet look.
2 No. So 1990s.
3 No. The benefits are far outweighed by the embarrassment factor.
4 Fine, and very relaxing, but in terms of physical results, unless one has the time and money to do it once a week, more effect can be had from the purchase of a lovely new dress or some excellent underwear. Best left to a girls' weekend away.
5 Yes, for those who live the kind of life whereby a manicure stays intact for more than about ten minutes.
6 Is one meant to talk to the therapist whilst having a facial, or pretend to be asleep? The key is to maintain a delicate state of suspended animation: do not talk, but at the same time make it clear that one is not asleep, perhaps by clearing one's throat occasionally, or even wriggling slightly.
7 Yes, especially for holidays when one has far better things to do of a bright, sparkling morning than spend an extra five minutes in the shower wrestling with a razor.
8 Yes, in moderation.
9 Makes all the difference. But beware of women with overly-thin eyebrows. They are not to be trusted.
10 Note, however, that a 'couple's massage' is never advisable as they are the very opposite of relaxing. Is one supposed to chat? Not chat? Look at each other? Not look at each other? It invariably leads to an uncontrollable giggling fit, and hence a perturbed, sometimes offended, massage therapist. Avoid.

The drinks party

The drinks party is without doubt the most challenging social battlefield of the new millennium. Whether it is birthday drinks down the pub or the launch of a new range of jewel-encrusted men's underpants at the Dorchester, the first few moments of these occasions tend to conform to few people's idea of a rollicking good time. Plunging headlong into a room full of acquaintances already all chit-chattering away at each other? Dancing around the difficulty of endless introductions? Eating standing up and with one hand? No thanks. But needs must, and as many of us become increasingly pressed for time, the drinks party has become the perfect way to squeeze numerous engagements into the same rainy Friday night. It is therefore important to find a way to negotiate them *with* charm and grace and *without* (too many) faux pas or (too much) falling over.

How to circulate

Where the circumference of the circle is approximately equal to sixty minutes.

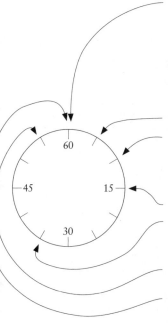

On arrival, tour the room. This is ostensibly an attempt to seek out the host or hostess, but is in actuality a form of reconnaissance. At certain parties, this activity is known as 'doing a celebrity circuit', which, should the occasion arise, is something to get over and done with as soon as possible. As a tactic, it is hugely preferable to the alternative, which is spending the entire evening looking over the shoulder of the person one is pretending to converse with in order to catch a glimpse of a more famous person standing nearby.

The host.

If single, the most attractive man or woman in the room; this should be a relatively brief chat, simply laying the groundwork for the actual pounce, which is best performed at the end of the evening. If not single – ditto, ideally, depending on the rational to irrational jealousy ratio of one's partner.

The guests one knows.

The guests one does not know (yet). Hopefully they will have had a bit to drink by now, thus facilitating the process of spouting nonsense that is integral to events of this kind.

The people in the loo (NB: For women, this is often the highlight of the evening.)

And begin again. Continue until the moment of departure looms, at which point the pounce first referred to at the ten-minute mark should be executed – ideally with care and precision, otherwise, simply with enthusiasm.

Ten common drinks-party pitfalls:

One: Failure to introduce. If in doubt, err on the side of recklessness – it is hugely preferable to introduce people who, it turns out, have known each other since they were born on the same day, in the same hospital ward, than not to introduce them at all. The latter is a horrible rudeness that is swiftly becoming the bane of the modern drinks party.

Two: Asking 'so, what do you do for a living?' within the first fifteen minutes of a conversation with a new acquaintance. To ask too early places you in the camp of the judgemental or the lazy. Not to ask at all, however, is not without its own risks, for one might merrily chatter away to someone for an hour about the weather, only to find out later that they were actually Johnny Depp's personal dresser. So after an appropriate length of conversational time has passed, the most acceptable ploy is to find a way to bring the subject up naturally.

Three: In an age where celebrity is all, it is not uncommon for the more cynical among us to be overly rude to this particular species, in a laudable attempt not to appear obsequious. The unfortunate result is that one ends up behaving in an even less friendly way than one would do to an unpleasant 'civilian' (in the unmatchable terminology of Elizabeth Hurley). So do try to act normal. And should one be desperate to talk to the celebrity, do not queue with the hoi polloi. It is so undignified. Wait until she or he is talking to just one other person, then approach. (At an office party, the same strategy applies for talking to the boss.)

Four: Should a celebrity merely be the topic of conversation, rather than actually present, hazards remain. There are some celebrities about whom it is acceptable to talk at any kind of gathering. These include Jennifer Aniston, Tom Cruise, Kate Moss and Madonna – in other words, the A-list. Girls Aloud are not such an inclusive subject, however. Celebrities also present an excellent recourse any time the conversation becomes too high-brow: there is little more fun to be had than asking the dean of a Cambridge college what he thinks of the new Robbie Williams album.

Five: 'Isn't it terrible what's happening in Chechnya?' 'Did you enjoy the latest Julian Barnes?' Both of these are conversational salvos designed to strike fear into the heart of the aural recipient, but stay calm. Try not to repeat the gist of an opinion piece from the previous day's newspaper, an all-too-common ploy. Instead, the key is to hark back to the past when answering: the past never changes, whereas the present often does, which is why staying up-to-date can be tricky. An acceptable response to 'Isn't it terrible what's happening in Chechnya?' might be something along the lines of, 'Well, it's always been a trouble spot, hasn't it? I mean, look at the 1830s: ever since Nicholas I invaded, it's been part of Russia's plan to expand southwards. I think it's the mountains . . .' then steer the conversation back to safer territory: a recent mountain-climbing holiday, the melting of mountains around the world as a result of global warming, or the many attractions of the Lake District, for instance. Similarly, a pertinent response to 'Did you enjoy the latest Julian Barnes?' might be 'It was his book before that that really blew me away.' An alternative approach, however, is simply to brazen it out – 'I've never read any Julian Barnes. Explain to me what it is about him that gets people so excited.' Remember: to be ignorant is fine, but to be fraudulent or pretentious is unforgiveable.

Six: It is unseemly to be seen to stuff one's face with food at a drinks party. This does not mean that food-stuffing cannot be done, however. One just has to employ a little stealth. During each conversation with someone new, limit oneself to eating just two of whatever delights are on offer. Then continue to circulate, and follow the same principle. *Et voilà,* a stomach full-to-bursting purely by dint of· playing the social butterfly.

Seven: In *Modern Manners* (Hamlyn, 1992), Drusilla Beyfus comments on one particular conundrum of the drinks party: how to disengage. She writes, 'No one is obliged to remain with the first people to whom they are introduced. A good moment for separation is when other people arrive to talk to someone else in the group. It would be oversensitive to feel miffed if people to whom you have been talking move on; it is quite in order for guests to wander off to pastures new with some casual observation such as 'I must have a word with Matthew over there' or simply, 'I'm going to circulate'. It is not necessary to make any excuse, however. Yet in practice, this can be a difficult course to steer. It is only the brave, rude or those with mild to severe Asperger's (which, to be fair, psychologists say is far more of us than one might think) who do not feel they ought to make some kind of attempt at an excuse. Everyone knows that it is an excuse, that one is not really going to get another drink, go to the loo or ask someone in the far corner of the room a terribly important question – but accepted social mores mean that no one would ever have the bad taste to acknowledge this. An alternative approach, however, is to say something along the lines of 'Right, I really ought to go and circulate I suppose, but may I take you with me?' – a simple but exceptionally charming way to disengage politely.

Eight: It is amazing how common it is to endure an entire drinks party without being asked a single question about oneself. Men of a certain type and age in particular tend to assume one has a boring job, especially if they know one is attending the said party with a partner who has an interesting job: the logic goes that for there to be *two* interesting jobs in one relationship is simply impossible, since how would there be any time to do the laundry? The appropriate response is to refuse to be cowed. Instead, as soon as there is a pause in the conversation, launch (*à propos* of nothing) into – 'I was on the *Today Programme* this morning' or 'George Clooney made love to me at lunchtime' or 'I'm a professional hot-air ballooner, have you ever tried it?' If the topic is interesting enough, few will remember the somewhat abrupt manner in which it was first introduced. And if they do, then at least it will have brightened things up a little: be provocative, be surprising, but never, ever be dull.

Nine: When Virginia Woolf lamented that 'Literature is strewn with the wreckage of men who have minded beyond reason the opinions of others', she could just as well have been talking about drinks parties. Nowhere else is the peculiarly human emotion known as embarrassment more frequently experienced. Some *faux pas* are avoidable: never ask someone if they are going to so-and-so's party next week, never ask someone if they are pregnant and never eat anything in public that resembles chocolate cake (it coats one's teeth so horribly easily). However, should an alternative metaphorical banana skin happen to present itself, remember that embarrassment is an emotion that is easily dealt with. The key is not to dwell on the hideous moment in question, but instead to pretend to oneself – vigorously, passionately and with true commitment – that the *faux pas* simply never happened. Train the brain to believe this; insist to the brain that it must believe this. Yes, it is a form of delusional behaviour; but a much-underrated one and one that really, truly works.

Ten: The trouble with drinks parties is that they instantly become less interesting, and less fun, the minute one is no longer on the lookout for sex. For this, let us be honest, is the *raison d'etre* of most such gatherings. The only solution is to leave early; and in doing so, be comforted by the fact that it is always more dignified to leave before the sun sets on a party – in other words, while it is still at its zenith. And, finally, accept that the most interesting conversations always take place just as one is getting one's coat. This is a fact of life, and is to be embraced.

The drinks party

Philosophy

....

The four main strains of Western philosophy

Ancient Greek philosophy: e.g. Socrates, Plato, Aristotle, Thales, Epicurus

Enlightenment philosophy: e.g. Kant, Hume, Descartes, Spinoza, Locke

Modern analytic philosophy: e.g. Wittgenstein, Russell, Frege, Quine, Rawls

Modern continental philosophy: e.g. Nietzsche, Marx, Sartre, Heidegger, Foucault

The acrimonious split between analytic and continental philosophy happened some time between the early nineteenth century and the early twentieth. It is one of those feuds where analytic philosophy remains bitter and resentful years later while continental philosophy is only vaguely aware that analytic philosophy still even exists.

Some questions that, contrary to popular misconception, philosophers rarely, if ever, ask

What is the meaning of life?
If a tree falls in a forest and there is nobody there to hear it, does it make a sound?
How can I calm down?

Not to be seated next to each other at a dinner party

A philosopher who has denied the existence of the mind: BF Skinner
A philosopher who has denied the existence of anything other than the mind: Plotinus

A philosopher who has denied the existence of God: Friedrich Nietzsche
A philosopher who has denied the existence of anything other than God: George Berkeley

A philosopher who has denied the existence of change: Parmenides
A philosopher who has denied the existence of anything changeless: Heraclitus

Five philosophy books that changed philosophy

1. Plato – *Republic* (c. 360 BC) – posed many of the questions that philosophy has been trying to answer ever since.

2. Aristotle – *Logic* (c. 350 BC) – provided tools for deduction that were not supplanted until the arrival of Gottlieb Frege (see below).
3. René Descartes – *Meditations* (1641) – posited that one can't be sure that anything exists except one's own mind.
4. Hume – *An Enquiry Concerning Human Understanding* (1748) – shattered many assumptions about science and epistemology.
5. Gottlieb Frege – *Begriffsschrift* (1879) – invented the modern system of predicate logic.

Five philosophy books that changed everything else

1. Confucius – *The Analects of Confucius* (c. 500 BC) – advice for living that has been followed in China for centuries.
2. John Locke – *Two Treatises of Government* (1689) – argues for the democratic rights that were later enshrined in the American constitution.
3. Karl Marx and Friedrich Engels – *The Communist Manifesto* (1848) – a call for revolution across the world.
4. Friedrich Nietzsche – *Beyond Good and Evil* (1886) – influenced everyone from the Nazis to the French Existentialists to The Doors.
5. Peter Singer – *Animal Liberation* (1975) – converted countless people into vegetarian anti-vivisectionists.

Five most impenetrable philosophy books

1. Immanuel Kant – *The Critique of Pure Reason* (1781) – argues that our experience of the world is mediated by mental concepts.
2. Georg Hegel – *The Phenomenology of Spirit* (1807) – explains how human consciousness evolves towards transcendence.
3. Bertrand Russell – *Principia Mathematica* (1913) – attempts to derive the whole of mathematics from logical principles.
4. Ludwig Wittgenstein – *Tractatus Logico-Philosophicus* (1921) – questions the relationship between language and reality.
5. Martin Heidegger – *Being and Time* (1927) – asks why there is something instead of nothing.

Five most depressing philosophy books

1. Niccolo Machiavelli – *The Prince* (1532) – argues that the best way to succeed in politics is to be utterly amoral.
2. Thomas Hobbes – *Leviathan* (1651) – argues that society would degenerate into savagery without an oppressive government.
3. Arthur Schopenhauer – *Essays and Aphorisms* (1851) – argues that suffering is an intrinsic part of the human condition.
4. Friedrich Nietzsche – *On the Genealogy of Morals* (1887) – argues that the very idea of being nice to others is a ploy by the weak to hold back the strong.

5. Guy Debord – *The Society of the Spectacle* (1967) – argues that everything in life is part of the inescapable hellish circus of capitalism.

Five most optimistic philosophy books

1. Plato – *Meno* (c. 380 BC) – argues that everyone is capable of knowledge and knowledge leads to virtue.
2. Epicurus – *Letters* (c. 310 BC) – 'Don't fear God, don't worry about death; what is good is easy to get, and what is terrible is easy to endure.'
3. Gottfried Liebniz – *Theodicy* (1710) – claimed (as satirised by Voltaire in *Candide*) that we live in the best of all possible worlds.
4. Georg Hegel – *The Phenomenology of Spirit* (1807) – predicted that humanity would ascend towards the transcendent knowledge that would reconcile us with the world and our own existence.
5. . . . is stretching it. Philosophy by its very nature is not a particularly optimistic pastime.

The approximate calorific value of various foodstuffs

An apple	72 calories
A banana	105 calories
A Mars Bar	230 calories
A bowl of cornflakes with semi-skimmed milk	200 calories
A chrysanthemum leaf	4 calories
A kumquat	13 calories
An ounce of raw acorns	109 calories
A small carton of popcorn, the kind one gets at the cinema that is most delicious when served as half sugar and half salt	400 calories
4.18400 joules, which is the quantity of thermal energy required to raise 1g of water by 1°C at 15°C	1 calorie[1]
1 kg of body fat tissue	7800 calories
A glass of champagne	89 calories
A pint of Guinness	170 calories

1 Also the definition of the term 'calorie', which comes from the Latin for 'heat', 'calor'.

A hot cross bun on Good Friday	205 calories
A delicious, crispy poppadom (with lime pickle)	90 calories
A Dungeness crab (cooked)	94 calories
An entire medium-sized roast chicken, with the skin	2142 calories
65 hard boiled eggs eaten in 6 minutes 40 seconds, which is the world competitive-eating record held by Sonya Thomas, a 39-year-old woman from Virginia (who weighs, incidentally, just 105 pounds)	5005 calories

In case of a genuine emergency

The likelihood or otherwise of many of the scenarios outlined below actually happening in our lifetime is widely disputed. As a result, the decision to stock the larder with fifty boxes of Bath Oliver biscuits and ten cases of bottled water is entirely a matter of disposition. But for those who would rather know than not know . . .

General instructions for any national emergency

Retreat indoors, and stay there until advised otherwise. Switch on the radio or television and wait to hear further instructions. Keep calm – mass panic can cause more injuries than anything else. Find out where and how to turn off water, gas and electricity supplies at home, the emergency procedures at the office or, for children, at school; how one's nearest and dearest plan to stay in touch, and if any neighbours need help. The more neurotically minded may also want to put together an emergency kit, either to sustain them through a few days holed up at home or to take with them in case of an evacuation. Suggested contents include:

- A first-aid kit, including any regular medication
- Some cash and a credit card
- A battery-powered radio with spare batteries
- A torch with spare batteries, as well as candles and matches
- A change of clothes
- A blanket

The approximate calorific value of various foodstuffs

- Non-perishable food and a tin opener
- Bottled water
- Dust mask, duct tape and plastic sheeting

In the event of . . .

A bomb explosion

If the explosion occurs outdoors, stay indoors (away from windows or doors) in case there is a second bomb in the area. If the explosion occurs indoors, evacuate by whatever route possible; if trapped, tap on pipes to try to make contact with rescuers. Do not strike matches – there may be a gas leak.

A chemical attack

Those in the vicinity of a chemical attack would suffer from nausea, blurred vision and/or breathing difficulties. Also keep an eye out for dead animals.

The priority is to find clean air as quickly as possible; hence, if the attack occurs outside, retreat indoors at once. Close all doors and windows and shut off any air-conditioning in order to halt the flow of air from outside. Then take shelter in an interior room, and seal it with plastic sheeting and duct tape if you can. Remain there until informed that it is safe to leave. If the attack occurs indoors, evacuate by whatever route possible; if trapped, open all windows and await help.

Once clean air has been found, it is essential to seek professional care. All clothing needs to be decontaminated and the body scrubbed thoroughly with soap and water to prevent any chemicals from spreading further.

A radiological attack (most probably in the form of a 'dirty' bomb)

This is initially difficult to identify. The bomb itself would be evident from the explosion, but it might be some time before it is identified as radioactive.

The priority is to avoid inhaling radioactive dust. To this end, follow the procedure described above for a chemical attack, but with one addition – cover the nose and mouth at all times. Also bear in mind that within twenty-four hours, the threat posed by this form of attack reduces dramatically. So try to sit it out.

A biological attack (for example anthrax or smallpox)

This can only be identified once other people start to show symptoms. These tend to appear flu-like at first, but within a few days become more recognisable – sufferers of smallpox, for instance, will develop a rash of flat, red spots which then turn into blisters.

If symptomatic, go to hospital. If not, minimise all contact with others.

A nuclear attack

This can be identified as such by a huge explosion, a blindingly bright flash of light, intense heat, and a mushroom cloud.

The priority is to avoid the radioactive fallout. To this end, if in the immediate vicinity of the blast it is essential to get out of the path of the radioactive cloud as quickly as possible. Ten minutes brisk walk should do it, but it is crucial to travel in the correct direction. Aim to move away from the centre of the blast, which is wherever the initial bright flash was seen or, failing that, where the most damage to buildings was done. Once this has been located, look up into the sky to see which direction the radioactive cloud is moving – in other words, which way it is being blown by the wind – then head off in a perpendicular direction. Keep going until out from underneath the cloud (which will not be as far as one might think, probably only a mile or so), then take shelter immediately to avoid being subjected to any residual radiation, as well as to continue to be protected should the wind cause the radioactive cloud to change direction.

If not in the immediate vicinity of the blast, seek shelter underground – in a basement, perhaps. It is imperative to protect oneself from the fallout with as much solid, dense material – such as concrete or earth – as possible. Even piles of books or newspapers will help. If there is nowhere underground to go, any building that is more than ten stories high will also do, but remain at least three stories from the top to avoid any radioactive material that falls on the roof. Stay there for at least forty-eight hours or until instructed that it is safe to leave (radioactive material decays quickly – up to 99 per cent after two days). If possible, decontaminate.

At all times, keep the nose and mouth covered.

An asteroid hitting the earth

Assuming there is some advance warning, which for an asteroid of any significant size there will be, the priority is to evacuate the area at risk. Otherwise, there is nothing personally one can do – except pray, possibly.

Aliens landing

Be friendly. One never knows what they might have to offer.

In case of a genuine emergency

How to get rid of guests at the end of a dinner party

··

While much has been written on the subject of receiving guests into one's home, there is, alas, precious little advice available on the subject of ejecting them. The dinner parties of today have the natural advantage of tending to take place in the evening, by which point many are already beginning to ponder the various pleasures that going home and crawling into bed hold. This was not always the case. In the Middle Ages, dinner was eaten at around 1 p.m., and it was only with the stirrings of industrialisation that the main meal of the day began to shift ever later – to 3 p.m. in the 1730s, 5 p.m. in the 1770s, 7 p.m. in the 1800s and 9 p.m. in the 1840s, a time around which it has fluctuated, by an hour or so each way, ever since. However, should the sheer lateness of the hour fail to persuade the assembled guests that it is time to wend their merry ways home, here are a selection of techniques designed to precipitate their departure, whilst causing minimum offence:

One: Do not supply guests with any stimulants, legal or otherwise, as this will only prolong the agony – the likes of coffee should be eschewed in favour of chamomile tea.

Two: If conversation should reach a natural lull, do not attempt to reignite it.

Three: Subtly cease refilling wine glasses and on no account open new bottles of anything.

Four: Start clearing the table and guests are very likely to leave – if only to avoid assisting in the washing up.

Five: Take a tip from pub landlords and make the surroundings subliminally less agreeable: brighten the lights; allow the room to become chilly by opening a window; put some challenging music on the gramophone.

Six: Once on your feet, remain standing; lingering by the door will politely suggest that it is time to go.

Seven: As a last resort, feign an altercation between you and your fellow host: an unseemly domestic incident will rid you of unwanted guests in a speedier fashion than anything else.

Woman

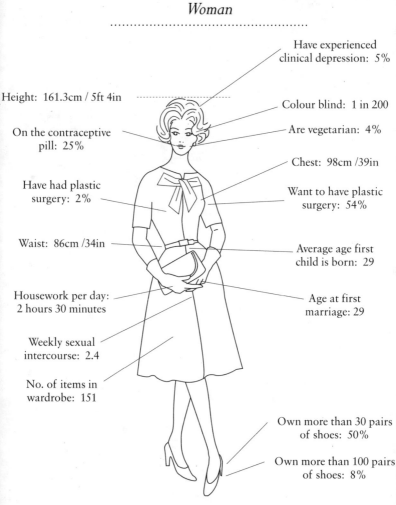

Have experienced clinical depression: 5%

Height: 161.3cm / 5ft 4in

Colour blind: 1 in 200

On the contraceptive pill: 25%

Are vegetarian: 4%

Chest: 98cm /39in

Have had plastic surgery: 2%

Want to have plastic surgery: 54%

Waist: 86cm /34in

Average age first child is born: 29

Housework per day: 2 hours 30 minutes

Age at first marriage: 29

Weekly sexual intercourse: 2.4

No. of items in wardrobe: 151

Own more than 30 pairs of shoes: 50%

Own more than 100 pairs of shoes: 8%

Weight: 69.4kg /153 lb

Life expectancy: 81 yrs
Median weekly earnings: £387
Age at which highest earnings are reached: 30–39
Voted in the last election: 61%
Have been to the moon: Zero